Building community information networks: strategies and experiences

Edited by Sheila Pantry OBE

Library Association Publishing
London

Published by
Library Association Publishing
7 Ridgmount Street
London WC1E 7AE

Library Association Publishing is wholly owned by The Library Association.

Published 1999

British Library Cataloguing in Publication Data
A catalogue record for this book is available from the British Library.

ISBN 1-85604-337-1

Typeset in 11/14 pt Bergamo and Autumn from author's disks by Library Association Publishing.
Printed and made in Great Britain by Bookcraft (Bath) Ltd, Midsomer Norton, Somerset.

Contents

The contributors

Graham Bagshaw

Graham Bagshaw is an IT consultant who specializes in computer networking, the Internet, and the development of IS/IT strategies. During most of his career he worked for the UK government, but since 1993 has run his own company. He first became interested in community networks in the early 1990s as a result of contact with the developers of the Canadian National Capital Freenet. Graham is a co-founder of SYNET and has been instrumental in setting up the Handsworth Community Information Site. He is a chartered engineer, and is a member of the Institution of Electrical Engineers and of the British Computer Society.

Graham Bagshaw, GB IT Services (Gbits)
Consultancy Services in Information Technology
PO Box 429, Sheffield S13 8YZ
UK
Tel: +44 (0)114 269 4333
Fax: +44 (0)114 269 4358
E-mail: graham@gbits.com
URL: http://www.gbits.com

Sheena Banks

Sheena Banks is currently Development Director of the Centre for the Study of Networked Learning in the Department of Educational Studies at the University of Sheffield. She was Director of the Dearne Valley Networked Learning Project from 1996–1998. She is involved in networked learning research and development, including transnational projects, at the University and is also involved in widening participation strategy. She is a member of the Advisory Board of the BBC Online Accreditation Project and has recently joined the editorial board of *Online access journal*. She was formerly Senior Lecturer in Enterprise at Manchester Metropolitan University and has extensive experience of managing innovation projects in HE.

Sheena Banks
Development Director
Centre for the Study of Networked Learning
Department of Educational Studies
University of Sheffield
Sheffield S10 2TN
UK
Tel: +44 (0)114 222 2000
E-mail: s.b.banks@sheff.ac.uk

John Dolan

John Dolan is Head of the Central Library in Birmingham, which is the largest public library in Europe with over two million visits per year. John has lead responsibility for Birmingham Library Services for strategic planning, research and marketing. He has been on secondment to the Library and Information Commission; he is project leader for the working group that prepared a report to government outlining the networking of public libraries in the UK.

John Dolan
Head of Central Services
Birmingham Public Library
Chamberlain Square
Birmingham B3 3HQ
UK

Tel: +44 (0)121 303 4511
Fax: +44 (0)121 233 9702
E-mail: JohnDolan@dial.pipex.com

Elenore Fisher

Elenore Fisher is currently Principal Librarian, Information Services, Rotherham Library and Information Services. She has worked in South Yorkshire public and college libraries since 1975, in a variety of posts – paid, voluntary, full and part time – with responsibilities ranging from mobile to reference services, library assistant to IT support. Since 1986, when she returned to Rotherham Pubic Library and Information Services, she has been involved in a range of projects which have the common aim of utilizing IT to provide a more efficient and effective service to colleagues and users alike.

Elenore Fisher
Information Services
Rotherham Library and Information Services
Walker Place
Rotherham
UK
Tel: +44 (0)1709 823 614
Fax: +44 (0)1709 823 650
E-mail: elenore.fisher@rotherham.gov.uk

Kevin Harris

Kevin Harris is Information Manager at Community Development Foundation and was Secretary to the INSINC Working Party. He has worked for 25 years in library and information work, in the public, private, academic and community sectors. He was previously a British Library Research Fellow and has worked for ten years at CDF where he manages the Information Unit and carries out development work in relation to public libraries and community applications of information technology. He was previously Secretary to ITaC, a working party on IT and Communities, which reported in 1992.

Kevin Harris
Community Development Foundation
60 Highbury Grove
London N5 2AG
UK
Tel: +44 (0)171 226 5375
Fax: +44 (0)171 704 0313
E-mail: kevin@cdf.org.uk

Mike Hosking

Mike Hosking is Head of Libraries and Information Services for Cambridgeshire County Council, Cambridgeshire. Libraries and Information has a very successful track record in obtaining development funding to enhance service delivery and provide new service options.

He has been involved with the Cambridge Online City since its foundation in 1996, and has been Chair of this community project for most of that period. Closely involved in the development of innovative use of information technology, he is very interested in the added value that community projects can add to more formal services provided by the local authority and others.

Mike Hosking
Head of Libraries and Information Services
Cambridgeshire County Council
Cambridge
Cambridgeshire
UK
Tel: +44 (0)1223 717063
Fax: +44 (0)01223 717079
E-mail: Mike.Hosking@libraries.camcnty.gov.uk

Helen Leech

Helen Leech has been working in public libraries in a range of authorities since 1989. In Essex, she was involved in the start-up and running of the community information project LIFE (Local Information for Essex). Since 1997 she has been working on CIRCE, a collaborative public library project looking at the feasibility of networking community information between public libraries across the UK.

Helen Leech
CIRCE Project Officer
Gloucestershire Library HQ
Quayside House
Gloucester GL1 2HY
UK
Tel: +44 (0)1452 425361
Fax: +44 (0)1452 425042
E-mail: hleech@gloscc.gov.uk
URL: http://www.gloscc.gov.uk/circe/

David Miller
David Miller works at the Department of Information Studies, Sheffield University. He has been working in the area of Community Information Networks (CINs) for the last five years. He has given numerous presentations and written papers on this topic. He is a member of SYNET who were the joint organizers of the first two Community Information Network conferences and a board member of UK Communities Online. He works with a number of groups who are at various stages in the development of their CINs.

David Miller
Computer Manager
Department of Information Studies
University of Sheffield
Regent Court
211 Portobello
Sheffield S1 4DP
UK
Tel: +44 (0)114 222 2644
Fax: +44 (0)114 278 0300
E-mail: d.miller@sheffield.ac.uk
URL: http://www.shef.ac.uk/~is/home.html

Michael Mulquin

After 11 years in church and community work in India and Pakistan, Michael moved back to the UK in 1986. He spent several years in race equality work in London before heading up the Community Involvement Unit, a community development team in East London. While there he gained European funding to set up the NewTel project which helps local voluntary organizations use the Internet to develop their work.

Since early 1995 he has been involved in promoting the use of Information and communications technologies to support local communities. He was first Chair, and then throughout 1998, full time Executive Director of Communities Online. Michael is now Director of IS Communications, a public affairs company specializing in Information Society issues. He is Chair of Newham Online and a board member of the European Association for Community Networking.

Michael Mulquin
Director, IS Communications
'Building the Information Society for citizens!'
2 Hertford Court
Vicarage Lane
East Ham
London E6 6BE
UK
Tel: +44 (0)181 552 7982
E-mail: michael@iscommunications.co.uk

Margaret Page

Margaret Page works independently, enabling partnerships in different countries and sectors to strengthen women's roles and initiatives in organizations. She has worked in community development, management education and the voluntary sector.

Marion Scott and **Margaret Page** jointly created Women Connect.

Marion Scott and Margaret Page
Joint Project Coordinators
WOMEN CONNECT

c/o CDF
60 Highbury Grove
London N5 2AG
Tel: +44 (0)171 226 5375
Fax: +44 (0)171 704 0313
E-mail: co-ord@womenconnect.org.uk
URL: http://www.womenconnect.org.uk

Sheila Pantry

Sheila Pantry has worked in information provision, including training of staff and users in a number of major industries. A move to the Health and Safety Executive provided the opportunity to establish and develop, over the period 1977 to 1993, the world renowned 'UK Health and Safety Executive Information Services'.

Sheila is very active in professional work both in the UK and internationally, particularly in developing information services based on computerised systems. Strongly committed to the use of computers in information dissemination and equality of access to information, Sheila is a co-founder of SYNET and has been involved in training, seminars and conferences. She was awarded the OBE for services to the health and safety information industry in 1993.

Sheila Pantry
Sheila Pantry Associates Ltd
85 The Meadows,
Todwick,
Sheffield S26 1JG
UK
Tel: +44 (0)1909 771024
Fax: +44(0)1909 772829
E-mail: SheilaPantry@compuserve.com
URL: http://www.silverplatter.com/oshinfo.htm

Marion Scott

Marion Scott promotes women's equality, creating new policy and practice in the public and voluntary sectors. She has worked in education, local government and the voluntary sector, as a manager of services and in a variety of roles.

Marion Scott and **Margaret Page** jointly created Women Connect.

Marion Scott and Margaret Page
Joint Project Coordinators
WOMEN CONNECT
c/o CDF
60 Highbury Grove
London N5 2AG
UK
Tel: +44 (0)171 226 5375
Fax: +44 (0)171 704 0313
E-mail: co-ord@womenconnect.org.uk
URL: http://www.womenconnect.org.uk

Artur Serra

Dr Artur Serra is working as a senior research scientist at the Universitat Politecnica de Catalunya in Barcelona, Spain, within the EPITELIO Project. His background is in anthropology. His research team is engaged in European research projects in the area of Computer Supported Cooperative Work (COMIC) Project. In 1993, they started Parrgea, the first Spanish national host of APC, an international network focused on giving telematic services to the NGOs. In 1996, they organized the first conference about the Internet and the Mediterranean, called InterMed. There they met Fiorella de Cindio and shared a common interest in community networking, especially in Southern Europe and the Mediterranean area. Artur is Coordinator of the Centre for Internet Applications (CANet) at the University.

Dr Artur Serra
Centre for Internet Applications, CANet.
Universitat Politecnica de Catalunya.
Campus Nord Gran Capita
s/n Modul D6-008
Barcelona 08034
Spain

Tel: +34 9 3401 7182
Fax: +34 9 3401 7055
E-mail: artur@ac.upc.es
URL: http://www.canet.upc.es

David Wilcox

David Wilcox worked both as a journalist and a consultant specializing
in community participation and partnership organizations before a visit
to the US in 1995 to meet community networkers inspired him to form
UK Communities Online with Michael Mulquin, Richard Stubbs and
others. He now helps create local networks and organizational intranets
through Partnerships Online, and facilitates connections between practitioners and policymakers through The Community Channel.

David Wilcox
Partnerships Online
13 Pelham Square
Brighton
BN1 4ET
UK
Tel/Fax: +44 (0)1273 677377
E-mail: david@communities.org.uk
URL: http://www.partnerships.org.uk
http://www.communitychannel.org.uk

Introduction

Introducing community information networks

SHEILA PANTRY OBE

Where did community information networks begin?

Community information networks (CINs) have been driven by the information and communication needs of local communities. In the past, there have been many ways in which communities have devised systems to communicate with each other, locally, national and internationally.

The European Commission (EC) has been working for some years encouraging the development of the 'Information Society'. Looking at the various EC programmes, we can see ones especially connected with community information networks, such as MBLN, which is a business opportunity for local newspapers.

Some of the principal reasons for the evolvement of CINs, or Free-Nets as they are known in the US and Canada, are far-reaching in their scope: achieving equality of access to information for all people – not a split society which is an information-rich versus information-poor society – so that individuals wherever they are located can achieve their potential, maximizing the economic benefits of any local, regional or national area.

Urgent concerns are being expressed by governments and those in the education sector that the skills needed by individuals and organizations will need to be rapidly upgraded to be able effectively and efficiently to perform jobs in the future.

The European Commission (EC) through its various directorates is pushing out a programme of lifelong learning for all citizens in Europe. This includes being competent in the use of information technologies (IT). The European Commission, Directorate General XIII on Information Society Technologies Content, Multimedia Tools and Market, otherwise known as ECDGXIII, has over the past few years in its work programme promoted projects which will help different industries to be ready and have staff trained to meet the demands of the future. It is through training in information technologies that people in the future will be able to gain quick access to the ever-increasing amount of information pertinent to their lives and jobs which is available via the Internet and other technology-based platforms.

The development of information provision and access

Up to now those seeking information do tend to rely heavily on their own print-based information collections, and also on information providers being able to produce and cope with the costs of the printed products.

Information centres and libraries recognized in the late 1970s that they could not cope financially with the avalanche of information in the traditional ways, and started to use the computer to produce databases and bring together local information.

As a result of the space programme, large-capacity computing power became available (eg through the European Space Agency), and offered to organizations opportunities to mount their databases on international services and online services accessible to anyone or any organization for a fee. The beginnings of an e-mail service were also offered and used as a way of quickly exchanging or requesting information from the other side of the world.

Electronic mail is one of the most compelling reasons for starting to use the computer to assist in our daily lives and work. We can quickly and cheaply send requests for information, and also store information in the electronic filing cabinets.

The Internet

Now in the 1990s the use of the Internet is offering everyone the opportunity not only to access information, but this time to make their own information available without going into print through the various journals and reports.

In many countries competent bodies are learning fast that the way to make information, particularly legislation, quickly available is to offer it on a website. We can see this happening in countries around the world, so it is becoming much easier to access the latest piece of information from countries where traditionally it may have been difficult to access the data. In the UK for the past two years we have been able to get the full text of each new piece of legislation 10 days after it has been passed in Parliament. And recently the European Commission has made the full text of its Official Journal available free of charge for 20 days after publication, so again it is easy to get the latest information on Directives etc. There are now many websites which are constantly being updated and enlarged. These are rich in content and make life so much easier for those wishing to have the latest information.

The only drawback, which no doubt will be improved, is that the search engines currently available do not have the technical sophistication of the online database systems and the CD-ROM services.

The IT and information skills needed

We know that the education sector needs to have money spent on it to enable both teachers and students become efficient and computer-literate. Therefore it will be some time before we have a workforce completely at ease with computerized information sources.

So it is incumbent on organizations and individuals to ensure that they have the necessary skills, both in understanding how information is produced and gathered together, and in retrieving the information. The training required for someone with basic computer skills should not take more than a day or two. Once these skills are learned it should be easy to cascade the knowledge within their own locality and workplace. This is particularly important as more and more small businesses are created not only in the UK but also worldwide.

But it is good to see governments, organizations and individuals recognizing that installing computers will aid the work flow and cut out some boring jobs, as well as providing access to information whenever they want it, and immediate access to Internet-based services such a electronic mail, websites etc at reasonable costs.

But the main question is how soon will people be sufficiently competent to be able to make best use of the available computerized up-to-date, authoritative and validated information sources?

Opportunities

Currently the technologies are rapidly expanding, and the equipment and telecommunications are becoming cheaper, enabling people for the first time to have their own computers and access a large range of information which has not been filtered by a particular media service.

About this book

This book brings together a number of different facets of community information networks. The chapters are written by individuals who have been working, sometimes since the early days, without knowing that others were pursuing the same goals. It has not been possible to have chapters on all the many and varied CINs which exist. Instead you will find a collection of stories of some of the variety of CINs which exist. To help with the terminology and understanding, David Miller has produced a chapter on definitions and a review of the developments. In Chapters 2 and 3, he has, using his vast experience, given a template on the steps necessary when creating a CIN. So why reinvent the wheel? Learn from others and avoid expensive mistakes. Therefore included are chapters on: the CIRCE research project, by Helen Leech; and the technologies available, what to avoid and what to use, by Graham Bagshaw. Kevin Harris describes how to nurture a community activity in the Information Society, and John Dolan shows how CINs and libraries and information services are so compatible.

There are various other models described: Artur Serra from Barcelona describes what is happening in a European city; Mike Hosking does the same for Cambridge – a very cosmopolitan city; Elenore Fisher describes the evolution of community information networks in a region, in contrast to Graham Bagshaw's very local CIN. Education for all is at the top of most people's agendas and Sheena Banks describes the Networks for learning experience. Women Connect, described by Marion Scott and Margaret Page, gives a view of a CIN for a specific group of people. Last but not least is David Wilcox and Michael Mulquin's description of building associations of CINs and bringing together all the various actors in the world of community information networks. The appendices also give a wonderful range of other CINs which are waiting to be contacted, together with further readings.

In the meanwhile readers from different backgrounds may be inspired to start and create a CIN of their own. The following ideas may appeal. The opportunities are endless, and it is hoped that this book will light a spark in the minds of those for whom a CIN would be a valuable asset.

Schools CIN

A CIN could be started by just one school or a group of schools in a locality. Again, there are many opportunities, not only to establish a CIN but also to reach outside of the school boundaries and offer opportunities to the 'computer terrified' to enable them to become 'computer literate'. At the same time, building such a CIN would help staff and pupils alike to develop and enhance their technological and communication skills. A good example of this type of CIN is the City School in Sheffield.

A local newspaper CIN

This CIN could be formed by the local newspaper wishing to make more of news opportunities. Or it could be established by a group of people in an information technology business wishing to offer their expertise. A good example of this is the Coventry and Warwickshire Network, which began life as the Coventry Community Network, now known and branded as CWN. As of January 1999 CWN was receiving over 35,000 visitors per month. It is updated daily with news and information about Coventry and Warwickshire. Since it started the site has had over 250,000 visitors who have read over one million pages and generated in excess of 10 million hits. CWN is nationally recognized as one of the largest and the most successful community information networks in Britain. It has been cited in numerous publications and has been demonstrated at many events across the country. It is nationally recognized as one of the only independent local news services on the web not to have originated from an existing press or media company, and is an excellent example for individuals and groups to follow.

Interest groups

There are many opportunities for interest groups, for example women, children, ethnic minorities, sports followers and people with other interests. Links can be made with similar groups elsewhere within the country, or even internationally, to share experiences and exchange information. An excellent example of this type of group is Women Connect.

Entrepreneur groups

Some CINs grow out of the ashes of unemployment in diminishing industries such as coalmining. GEVH Ltd (Grimethorpe Electronic Village Hall) was started as an interest group by some redundant mine workers, who now, after three years, have a limited company which offers commercial website services as well as training at all levels of the computer skills spectrum.

Public libraries and local CINs

There are numerous different types of community information network based within public libraries, or within groups which are encouraged and supported by them. These sites can cover a wide range of subjects and interests, such as:

- historic connections
- church and religious connections

- shops, hotels and pubs
- local sports, over 60s, scouts, cubs, brownies and environment groups
- diary of local events
- ex-patriot's page, which can be used as a forum connecting ex-residents of the locality
- schools and the facilities they offer
- entertainment in the locality.

There are many good examples of these types of CINs.

Conclusion

One of the ideas in bringing together this book was to share experiences with others who may be thinking of starting a CIN, to benchmark where we are at present as we approach the Millennium, and most of all to show that networks and networking – whether public or personal – do work, and are really helping to close the information-rich versus information-poor divide. Through the examples described, the authors show that it is possible for many different types of people to come together and produce a community information network of their own, often, in the beginning, without financial aid or even computer skills.

I hope that this book will inspire those who know that they could and should be producing their own CIN, and let them know that there are many people available now with the energy, experience and enthusiasm to help get them started.

1

Community information networks
Definitions and a review of the developments during the 1990s

DAVID MILLER

During the development of community networks there have been a number of attempts to produce definitions to help provide an understanding of what they are and how they are perceived around the world. The following also illustrates the problems faced, and the current challenges to be met for community networks to survive.

What's in a name?

Morino[1] (1994) lists the following synonyms for community networking: civic networking, community bulletin boards, community computing, community information systems, community telecomputing and telecommunity systems. Perhaps the terms Free-Net and CivicNet should also be added to this list. Morino then goes on to define community networking as

> . . . a process to serve the local geographical community – to respond to the needs of that community and build solutions to its problems. Community Networking in the social sense is not a new concept, but using electronic communications to extend and amplify it certainly is.

Beamish[2] in 1995 defines community networking as

> . . . a network of computers with modems that are interconnected via telephone lines to a central computer which provides: community information; and a means for the community to communicate electronically.

The National Public Telecomputing Network,[3] defines a Free-Net as follows:

> They are multi-user systems with much of the power and sophistication of a commercial online service like CompuServe. Yet each system is locally owned, locally operated, and designed to wrap itself around the information needs of the community.
>
> Any user with a personal computer and a modem can dial into these systems, 24 hours a day, and access the information and communication services found there.
> - Free-Nets are driven by the information and communications needs of the local community.
> - Their governance and organisational roots are in the community itself.
> - They are dedicated to bringing the benefits of the Information Age to as many people as possible, at the lowest possible cost.

In addition to the provision of local information to a local community there are two further aspects to examine when defining a community information network:

1 The use of the network as an 'on-ramp' in terms of Internet access and usage by the local community. Once users become familiar with the system for finding local information, they are in the position to explore further afield for other Internet resources.
2 The community network will also serve to attract 'virtual visitors' to the community, and can be used as a tool for marketing the town and its products.

Distinguishing characteristics

While each community network is unique, they do share a number of common characteristics that differentiate them from other types of networks.

Local

As a general rule a community network is developed by the people in a community, contains information relevant to people within the community, and uses information provided by members of the community. The network aims to improve the flow of information to its intended audience and to facilitate discussion on local issues. Both the network information providers and the people accessing their information come from all sectors of the community – local government, education, business, community groups and individuals. An essential element for success is that these networks should be controlled by the grassroots community and not as 'infrastructure'. These networks should be caretakers of electronic public space created *by* the community, not providers of something *for* the community.

Access

The Morino Institute[4] (1995) stated that 'Unless every individual, organization and community has access to interactive communications and the opportunity it offers, the new Communications Age will never realise its potential and society will be the poorer.'

The Morino Institute also stated, in the same report that access to interactive communications should be 'as common, affordable and essential as the availability of electricity was in the industrial growth of the United States in the 20th Century'.

This is a view very much shared by the initiators, developers and managers of community networks.

One of the most important features of any community network is the effort that goes into ensuring ubiquitous access to the system. There are a number of different models that community networks can adopt, but irrespective of the model, there will be a determination to ensure access is available to each and every member of the community. This may involve provision of public access terminals for those who do not have computers at home; these may be placed in public libraries, unemployment centres and so forth. Another feature is free access to some members of the community through subsidized or free telecommunications. The major concern is that, unless equal access is offered to all members of the community, existing gaps between the social classes will be widened through the emergence of 'information-rich' and 'information-poor' classes. ImpactOnLine, an American non-profit organization which aims to offer computer education and access to those lacking such resources, makes the following observations:[5]

> The explosion of hype and hyperbole surrounding the Internet has not occurred without casualty. Lost in the giddy hope for a system of ubiquitous information and entertainment is the reality that this new system will never be universal. The information infrastructure that the Internet and other systems are helping to build are based on computer and communication technologies.

This structure poses two problems:

1   Computers cost money;
2   A large portion of our society does not have money.

Steve Glikbarg[6] comments

> The Internet represents a luxury that only a few can afford, yet knowledge of its technology and culture is quickly becoming a necessary skill for today's world. It is already accepted fact that general computer skills are a necessity for today's youth, but again, access to the required resources are not ubiquitous.
>
> Our new 'Information Age' is slowly developing two new classes of society: the information rich and the information poor. In this classic case of the 'haves' and the 'have-nots', we aim to help those who need it most.

On this side of the Atlantic the British Labour Party[7] has this to say:

> But we acknowledge that there will always be those who cannot afford to link their own home into the communications networks, and we must ensure that such people do not become 'information-poor' and sharply discriminated against as a result . . . Technology has the power to empower and free individuals and enrich their communication with the state; it also has the power to become an oppressive and divisive tool creating new classes of information rich and poor.

Goals of community networks

Economic regeneration

Many of the existing community networks have been set up with the aim of improving the lot of disadvantaged communities. Areas where unemployment is high, and where traditional industries had been to the forefront, are turning towards newer technologies in the hope of turning the tide of unemployment and attracting new industries to their communities.

The examples of Ipswich City, near Brisbane in Australia, and Blacksburg Electronic Village, Virginia, highlight this point. In Ipswich City unemployment has been a major regional issue since the mid-1980s. In a talk given at AusWeb 95, Balson, the manager of the Ipswich project explained the city's background as one where there had been a coal mining industry, a railway workshop, engineering works, meat preservation plants, woollen mills and brick works. By the mid-1980s Ipswich was facing high unemployment following the demise of these traditional industries. Balson[8] goes on to describe the choices they made:

> The City Council had a choice of trying either to woo new rust bucket industries or to replace the dying coal and manufacturing industries with new emerging industries . . . the City embarked on a major project to change the focus of employment into smart industries based around a smart community.

The project is now being run by a series of small community-based groups who are concerned with areas of the project. Education, culture and business, for example, have been split and are being managed by people with the relevant knowledge and interests.

Similarly, in Blacksburg, Virginia, USA, employment was dependent on natural resource industries and heavy manufacturing and the town faced a rise in unemployment on their decline. Beamish[2] comments:

> The town believes that technology and communications will be the driver of future economic growth in the region and consequently want an extensive high-speed, two-way information network in Blacksburg. They

believe that a network accessible by the entire community is a core to the information society.

Many of the community networks are too new to be judged in terms of success or failure, but certainly there are individual stories that attest to the success of the Internet as a communications tool. The Morino Institute[4] also comments:

> . . . we believe that the local community is where our toughest social problems – crime, inadequate education, underemployment – will be solved, by the grass- roots efforts of the people who have the most personal stake in their solution. It is here that community networking takes on such relevance in helping people solve problems and addressing the needs of their day-to-day lives.
>
> Clearly, community networking is an emerging phenomenon with the potential to effect profound societal transformation.

Establishing a sustaining economic model

Morino[1] argues that community networks must generate some funds from charging fees for some of its services and also from long-term, guaranteed sources of funding. It need not necessarily be self-funding, and the network can avail itself of grants and other such moneys, but should not be dependent on this type of funding for its survival.

Sources of funding

With regard to sources of funding for community networks there are two types of funding to take into consideration, namely the initial set-up funding and the ongoing funding. There are a number of sources of funding for community networks; some examples are:

- individual users through their subscriptions
- local businesses through cash donation, sponsorship and passing-on of redundant equipment
- national or international companies through sponsorship or donation of their goods or services

- local, national and international grants
- schools, colleges and universities that work with the community.

Other options according to Morino[1] would include:

- a commitment to long-term funding by an organization
- building the cost of the network into the local tax system so that like the traditional structure of the local library the network is 'free'.

Challenges to community networks

The first challenge is keeping the momentum going. Often community networks are founded by one or a few volunteer members of the community, who work from their own homes in many cases. Once the number of users is increased, however, more formal structures will need to be involved, and full-time staff recruited. Morino[1] comments:

> Community networks, once they achieve certain levels of success or critical mass, must have a formal 'infrastructure' and full time staff. The pioneers of community networking have done incredible, absolutely unbelievable work . . . This model will continue to work for small systems that remain satisfied with a relatively narrow focus – but it clearly will not hold for most community networks and the demands they will face.

Challenges are:

- lack of stable funding – they are often forced to operate on a day-to-day basis as they are not sure of long-term funding
- increasing expectation of users – users increasingly seeking more from the service as they become familiar with the service and look for additional services and products.

Community networking in the UK

There is now an expansion in the number of CINs at various stages of development in the UK (a listing is available at **http://panizzi.shef. ac.uk/community**) and we can begin to offer a typology of such systems. They may be initiated and developed by different interests:

The local authority

These can be seen as a development of the earlier video-text type systems, where the information is provided and controlled by a central administration and the user is perceived as a 'passive recipient' of the information provided. This type of system aims to provide information on the services provided by the authority, as an extension of information also made available in 'dead tree' format. Funding for these CINs usually comes from the local authority central budget.

Private-sector initiatives

Some small local internet companies see a commercial advantage in developing CINs and seek to provide such information as a way of attracting visitors to their website. These systems are usually funded by advertising revenue. Also in this category are the systems initiated by the economic regeneration agencies (City Challenge etc), which aim to provide such systems as a way of assisting in the economic regeneration of the region.

User-led initiatives

These are a new and exciting development. These systems are characterized by a user-led, 'bottom-up' development, with an initial 'technology-led' drive. A group of enthusiasts from various sectors of the local community, who perceive the benefits of a CIN, and understand the potential use of the Internet as a delivery mechanism, join together to form partnerships with other local information providers and users with the aim of providing a local information service. One of the many challenges facing CINs of this type is the securing of long-term funding to ensure a sustainable and developing future.

It is in this third type of CIN that the most innovative and exciting developments are taking place. Cross-sector partnerships are being developed which bring benefits, both economic and social, and allow for the active participation of the total user population. The information content available on such systems is owned and controlled by the providers themselves, as opposed to being mediated through a third party, and the providers are responsive to the requirements of the user population.

All of the CINs of this third type are in the early stages of development. Different CINs have different sets of partners and different forms of 'ownership', some charitable-based and some as public limited companies. There are many models of development of CINs of this type, but they can be seen to have a similar set of 'core values' around the issues of 'openness', 'access' and 'participation'. Many of the more forward-looking local authorities and regeneration agencies are actively supporting the development of CINs of this type as a way of servicing their own information provision requirements and ensuring community participation.

Developments of this type form the basis of the Information Society. They allow and encourage the active participation of individuals as part of the local community and thus as part of the wider community. They provide a vehicle for the provision of training and support in the skills required to operate successfully in this new society. They aim to be inclusive and thus address the issues of 'information-rich versus information-poor'. They give a concrete reality to the oft-expressed need to ensure that individuals from all levels of society are the beneficiaries of the development of the Information Society.

References

1   Morino, M, *Assessment and evolution of community networking* (paper presented at 'Ties that Bind' Apple Computer/Morino Institute Conference 'On Building Community Computing Networks', 5 May, 1994), Apple Computer, Cupertino, CA, 1994. Available at
    <http://www.cais.com/morino/htdocs/ties94sp.htm>
2   Beamish, A, *Communities on-line: Community based computer networks* (MSc Dissertation), Cambridge, MA, 1995. Available at
    <http://alberti.mit.edu/arch/4.207/anneb/thesis/toc.html>
3   National Public Telecomputing Network, *Starting a Free-Net®*, Community Computer System, 1995. Available at
    <http://www.nptn.org:80/about.fn/starting.fn>

4   The Morino Institute, *Doors of opportunity for local communities*, Reston, VA, 1995. Available at
     <http://www.cais.com/morino/htdocs/pandintr.htm>

5   Glikbarg, S, Impact OnLine. Available at
     <http://www.Impactonline.org/>

6   Glikbarg, S, *Cookin' on the net*, 1995. Available at
     <http://www.nrh.com:8400/cookinover.html>

7   British Labour Party, *Communicating Britain's future Labour's information superhighway policy*, 1997. Available at
     <http://www.poptel.org.uk/labour-party/policy/infohighway/index.html>

8   Balson, S, Global Info-Links and the smart city. In Debreceny, R S and Ellis, A E (eds), *Innovation and diversity: the World Wide Web in Australia: AusWeb95: Proceedings of the First Australian World Wide Web Conference*, Lismore, NSW, Norsearch Publishing, 1995.

2

Establishing a community information network
The way forward

David Miller

Introduction

The purpose of this chapter and Chapter 3 is to outline the steps that should be taken and the further actions necessary to develop a community information network (CIN). They outline the aims and objectives of the project, set out a 'template' for the initial project proposal, and give suggestions for the various work packages needed to bring the project to a successful conclusion.

The aim of the project is to develop a community-based electronic information network based on models of community networks in the UK, Canada and the US. This will involve the provision of community information, ensuring access to this information, and providing training and support in the use of the network.

The steps involved in the successful completion of the project are examined, a number of proposals for a phase two of such a project are put forward, and recommendations in relation to these options are made.

The project should be set out using a phased approach, and the main phases of the project are outlined as follows:

Phase 1 – establishing the vision

The initial time scale of such a project should be approximately three to four months and it should consist of a number of different tasks:

- providing an initial community website
- analysing the requirements of the user base in the community
- 'awareness raising' in the community, involving the commercial, public and community sectors
- identification of potential partners for phase 2 of the project.

Phase 2

The aim of this phase of the project is to develop a community-based electronic information network based on models of community networks in the UK, Canada and the US. This will involve providing community information, and access to this information. Access would need to be provided from both public 'community information points' (eg local branch libraries, schools, public offices etc) and private offices and homes.

The details of this phase, and the development of the proposal, would be a responsibility of the partnership formed in phase 1. Phase 2 may last for 18 months to two years and involve the full-time employment of at least one person.

Phase 3

This phase will take the form of the hand-over of the project from the initiating organization to the community in the locality. By this stage a solid user base will have been established, and an 'organization' to maintain and take the project forward will have been developed. The initiating organization would hand over the project to the community and envisage providing some continuing support and advice over a three- to six-month period.

One of the tasks of the individual(s) employed would be the identification of other sources of funding (eg the EU) and applying to such sources for further funding.

Project aims and objectives

The aim of the project is the development of a community information network. The objectives of the project are to develop a network within the existing community that will fulfil the following criteria:

1   The community information network will provide the community
    with information pertaining to many organizations, services and
    products in the community in an easy-to-access and readily available
    format. The network will improve the flow of information and
    communication amongst its intended users.
2   The project will aim to ensure equal access to information for all
    persons in the community. The project must ensure that existing
    social gaps are not further emphasized by the introduction of
    information technologies. To this end the provision of hardware,
    physical locations for public information access points, and training
    and support in the use of the network, should form part of the
    project outline.
3   It is expected that, through the use of the community information
    network, the people in the area will be then be in a position to
    transfer the skills developed in order to take full advantage of the
    potential offered by the electronic information age.
4   The local information should also be accessible on the Web,
    because the potential 'audience' for a set of World Wide Web pages
    is not restricted to either the locality or the UK, but is, as the name
    suggests, worldwide in scope. Consequently, it represents, for
    business and other sectors of the local community, an opportunity
    to market services and products on a worldwide basis. A well-
    developed and actively promoted presence on the Internet can only
    be beneficial to the economic regeneration of the area.
5   In addition to the economic aspect of an Internet presence, the
    project will present a positive image of the town and its people to
    the world at large.

Designing a project: phase 1

Before any discussion is made of the project is it important to examine
the background to the project idea. There are a number of factors that
will lead to the decision to develop a community network:

1   **To assist in economic regeneration**. With the closures of major

industries (eg coal mines) and a number of other businesses in an area, there is a high rate of unemployment.

In their report *Confronting industrial demise*, Halstead and Wright[1] questioned approximately 200 miners and their families. The miners hailed from Yorkshire, Derbyshire and Nottinghamshire, and 19% of the total were from Barnsley. Of the total, 90.9% were no longer employed by British Coal. According to the report, 56.7% of respondents from Barnsley had been successful in finding a new job.

2   **To develop new skills within the community**. It is vital, with the demise of the more traditional industries, that the community in a particular area should keep up to date with the ever-growing range of information products.

> . . . yet knowledge of its technology and culture is quickly becoming a necessary skill for today's world. It is an already accepted fact that general computer skills are a necessity for today's youth . . .[2]

3   **Knowledge of the development of such networks in other countries**. As has been outlined in Chapter 2, community networking has been operating successfully, primarily in the US and Canada, for some years.

4   **The growth in the development of such networks in the UK**. The growth in popularity of the World Wide Web has resulted in an explosion of activity in UK local authorities, educational establishments and businesses to get a place on the Internet.

5   **A bid to encourage inward investment from the business and tourist sectors**. The World Wide Web will act as a promotional tool for a town.

The aims of the first phase of a project should be to ensure the successful completion of these various strands of the project:

* the development of an initial World Wide Web site
* the completion of a survey of the needs and requirements of the area's various sectors
* 'awareness raising' in the community, especially in the business and

local government sectors

- the identification of potential partners for phase 2 of the project.

The development of an initial World Wide Website

If no presence exists on the Internet, one of the first tasks to be completed will be the design and authoring of the initial suite of web pages representing the CIN. Negotiations should be simultaneously ongoing with local authorities regarding the provision of information. The information input to the web pages is information that is currently publicly available in printed form, or information provided by the organization. Some of it may be of a reasonably static nature, ie not requiring updating on a constant basis.

The pages could be structured under under a number of main headings as outlined below:

1 **Local authority**
   Key facts, maps and pictures of the town or area in general, the town or parish hall, the council (structure, political make-up, wards and councillors, parliamentary constituencies and council officers), and council activities and services.

2 **Business**
   - economic agencies: this section lists and will detail the various agencies and their services
   - companies: at present details similar to that found in a directory; companies will be offered the opportunity to take further space to provide more product/service or company details
   - business websites: at present a list of agents in the area that handle business websites
   - links to sites offering information on business grants available in the UK and in the EU.

3 **Education**
   This section should cover the local education authority, libraries and information services, primary schools, secondary schools, further education and special schools.

4 **What's on guide**
   Including details of parks, farms, nature reserves, museums, gal-

leries, historic/industrial buildings and monuments, cinemas, walks, night-clubs, shopping, leisure and special events, places to eat and places to stay.

5   **Public sector**
This section of the pages offers free presence on the WWW to the following types of organizations: careers advice services, charitable organizations, charity shops, children's homes, citizens' advice bureaux, clubs and associations, community centres, consumer organizations, counselling and advice services, information and services for the disabled, environmental groups, family planning centres, helplines, religious groups and places of worship, social service and welfare organizations, voluntary organizations, and youth and community groups.

Letters should be written to these organizations requesting information regarding their services and explaining the project to them. They should be asked to supply information that they are agreeable to make available on the Internet.

6   **People**
This section will be where individuals or groups can opt to take space to set up their personal home pages.

Analysing the requirements of the user base

A survey of the business community

A survey of businesses involved should be carried out. Personal interviews should be conducted with a sample of companies with 100 or more employees, and a postal questionnaire could also be sent to representative samples of companies with less than 100 employees.

Personal interviews

An initial contact letter should be sent, followed by a telephone call requesting an interview. This interview will clarify any points which will be useful for the whole survey.

Nowadays a majority of companies will be aware of the Internet, and some of them may be currently using it for business purposes. Current knowledge of the Internet will come from the media – TV, newspapers and radio. Also, computer journals are a source of information regarding the Internet. These journals may be seen as a source of further information and information relating to specific enquiries.

Many companies will intend to use the Internet as a sales tool, and may need to be able to update the pages regularly, and also to be able to maintain control of their pages. One of the advantages of the Internet is the capability of having information that is correct and completely up to date. Training with regard to writing their own pages may also be needed. Their aim generally will be to maintain and update their own pages but not necessarily the initial design of the pages. Some of the companies will be interested in designing their own site.

Newspapers

It will be worth contacting local newspapers interested in setting up as an electronic newspaper provider, and these may already have in-house server facilities that could be utilized.

Postal survey

Response to a postal survey may offer some indication of potential local involvement. Beware of sending out postal surveys at holiday times, because the response rate will be low.

If the survey reveals that businesses are not yet using the Internet, it may be opportune to hold a meeting and demonstrations to reveal the opportunities available. Some negative responses may be received.

For those either not sure about the use of the Internet, or planning to use the Internet the following purposes could be given:

- public relations
- competitor information
- customer support
- marketing
- direct sales
- staff recruitment

- information access
- increased competitiveness
- increased sales/market share
- presence in a world-wide market
- enhanced communications
- ability to view competitors.

Other business benefits are:

- access to technical information
- access to information about potential clients and customers.

The following functions may be used:

- electronic mail
- file transfer
- World Wide Web
- database searching.

Awareness raising within the community

A large proportion of the work to be carried out for the establishment of a CIN will involve raising awareness levels about the Internet and the potential for electronic communications in general and the project in particular within the various strands of the community. This will involve contacting individuals and groups by mail and in person, such as:

1 **Members of Parliament**
   Letters should be sent to the local MPs, giving details of the project and offering space for their own web page.
2 **Councils**
   If the project is not backed by the local authority, then letters should be sent out to all the local councillors and heads of the council departments.
3 **Education, information services and libraries**
   - a meeting should be arranged with the local information services and libraries

- colleges should also be contacted; if there are a number in the area, perhaps a separate meeting should be arranged.

4   **Business agencies and businesses**

The survey itself will have raised the awareness of the business community for the project and, it is believed, the Internet in general. Some of the respondents to the survey may request further information on the project and on the Internet in general, so be prepared to have some information ready – a 'frequently asked' fact sheet may be a useful thing to compile.

In other projects the personal interviews have proved successful in raising awareness for the project and resulted in a number of further visits by the companies to view both the project's pages and other Internet sites of interest to the company.

There should be a number of meetings with members of the business support agencies in the area. The Chamber of Commerce could be contacted to provide a letter of support for the project which could be sent out to companies along with the questionnaire.

5   **Non-profit sector**

Letters should be sent out to members of the voluntary and non-profit sector to inform them about what is being done, and to offer them free space to promote themselves and their services. There should be a significant number of favourable replies with information to be placed on the Internet.

6   **Community groups**

Existing community groups in the area should be contacted and meetings held to explain the project.

Identification of potential partners for phase 2 of the project

As a direct result of raising the levels of awareness in the community, parties who are interested in the project and in seeing it through to fruition will begin to emerge. Interested parties will be very much representative of the entire community – business, economic agencies, local government, education, the non-profit sector and community groups.

The initial intention is to bring together the interested parties in a general meeting to formulate the plan for phase two of the project.

The succesful completion of phase 1 of the project will have the following outcomes:

- an initial World Wide Website will have been established
- a survey of local businesses will have been conducted
- awareness-raising of the opportunities afforded by the Internet.
- the project partnership for phase 2 will have been established.

With this background, and now that the 'ownership' of the project has been widened, the move to phase 2 can take place. This is described in Chapter 3.

References

1   Halstead, J and Wright, P, *Confronting industrial demise*, University of Sheffeld, Division of Adult Continuing Education and Rotherham Metropolitan Borough Council Department of Planning. 1995.

2   Glikbarg, S, *Cookin' on the net*, 1995. Available at **<http://www.nrh.com:8400/cookinover.html>**

3

Establishing a community information network – phase 2
Developing the vision

DAVID MILLER

Introduction

One of the reasons for operating the project in a phased manner is to ensure that, before a full-scale community network is planned, there is shown to be sufficient interest among the various sectors of the community. During the course of phase 1, representatives of the various sectors will have been approached and it is should be apparent if there is support for the development of a community network in the area.

Aims and objectives of phase 2

The aim of phase 2 of the project, which should be expected to last for two years, is the development of the organization or structure that will ensure the viable long-term future of the project.. This will involve a decision-making process on what type of structure is best geared to fulfil the aims and objectives of the programme.

In order to fulfil this aim, the following factors are of critical importance and will be fully examined in this report (phase 2 aims to determine a combination of these factors, such that they are acceptable to all the sectors of the community):

- web server
- access to information
- information provision

- community involvement.

Program options

There are a number of different structures that might be adopted in phase 2 of the project, the selection of which will be based in part on the choices made in relation to the issues outlined above. The different program options will carry different levels of cost and reward for the community.

Commercial venture

The project could be run by a commercial enterprise, either existing or set up specifically to run the project.

In this scenario the company would almost definitely require its own server, in order to generate income by selling space on its server to companies outside the area. Also, the organization could act as an Internet provider offering access both to members of the community and to any interested individual.

Type of funding required:
The project would require initial start-up funding, but would be intended to turn a profit within a set time frame.

Advantages:
- no long-term financial commitment required
- potential for income generation; could be in the form of selling server space, authoring web pages or offering Internet access.

Disadvantages:
There is a danger that, if forced to operate on a for-profit basis, the company might forsake the aims of the project in terms of equal access for all the community, and instead focus on the more lucrative sectors of the community, namely the business sector, to the exclusion of other sectors.

Public operation

If this type of structure were to be adopted, the project would eventually be taken over by an existing public body that would ensure long-term funding for the project.

Type of funding required:
Start-up and guaranteed long-term running costs.

Advantages:
This structure would be able to offer access to all as its purpose would not be to make a profit.

Disadvantages:
- funding would be long-term and would require a formal and long-term commitment
- public bodies are subject to reorganization and structuring, and this could result in problems regarding ownership and management of the project.

Charitable trust

The venture could be run as a form of a charitable trust and would in many ways be a combination of the above two options.

The project would be self-funding. A commitment would have to be made funding to a certain level, or for a certain time frame, assuming that the project might not be immediately self-funding.

Type of funding required:
It would require start-up funding and some income stream.

Advantages:
It could offer free access to some and charge others to ensure funding from the sectors who could afford to pay while conversely ensuring access to those who could not afford to pay.

Disadvantages:
- would need some guaranteed ongoing funding, at least for a certain

time period
- potential conflict over free versus paid-for access.

Full examination of the options

The factors listed in the aims and objectives for phase 2 will be examined here in further detail to demonstrate the importance they play in the selection of a structure to manage the project. The four factors are interlinked to an extent, and the choice made with regard to one can favourably or adversely affect the others, as will be illustrated.

The setting-up of the business will be looked at in a number of work packages, detailing their aims, timescales and deliverables.

Web server

The choice here lies between whether to purchase a server specifically for the use of the project, or to use an existing server from within the community, or to 'buy in' storage space.

The issues to be examined in relation to this decision (see Table 3.1) are initial set-up costs, running costs, the potential to generate income and the management of the information (ie adding, removing or updating information).

Table 3.1 *Issues affecting the choice of web server*

	Own server	Renting space
Set-up costs	high	low
Running costs	high	low
Income generation	possible	not possible
Information management	easier	more difficult

The possibility of using a server that is already located in the community has not been included in Table 3.1, as different conditions might exist depending on the choice of server. In general, though, the set-up cost would not be expected to be as high as the cost of purchasing a server. Also, the running costs would be lessened if there was an existing systems operator, familiar with the server. Issues regarding income generation and information management would have to be decided between the two parties.

Internet access

The issues to be examined with regard to Internet access are

- the general procedure for connecting to the Internet
- how to offer the community access to the network
- how to ensure that all members of the community can have access to the community network.

The general procedure for connecting an individual to the Internet

The first thing needed to connect to the Internet is a computer. The type depends on the software chosen, but the most common is a Windows-compatible computer.

A modem will be needed to connect your computer to your phone line. The choice of modem will revolve around the issues of speed and price, and the faster the modem the more expensive it will be.

Internet access through an Internet services provider will be needed, and there are very many of these to choose from. Pipex has a list of Internet service providers (**http://www.limitless.co.uk/inetuk/ providers.html**) with details of such companies. The prices charged by these providers will vary depending on the level of service they provide. The method of charging is as variable as the prices.

Some providers will make an initial set-up charge. They can then either have set charges for specified periods of time, charge by the connect hour or minute, or provide a free connection.

In addition to this, users will have to pay their own telephone charges; calls are charged at a local call rate.

Most Internet service providers offer free and unlimited e-mail facilities as part of the subscription. However, there are a number that charge for e-mail, either by charging a set price per month, or by providing a certain number of e-mails free, or by charging according to the size of the e-mail. A number of free e-mail services are available via the

World Wide Web which can be used to access e-mail from any computer connected to the Internet.

Internet access software will also be needed. This is readily available from a range of different suppliers, and most Internet service providers will supply a form of this software.

How to offer Internet access to the community

The first decision is how to offer access to the Internet. There are three possible routes that the project can follow:

- becoming an Internet provider and offering direct Internet access to the community
- 'buying in' the service from an existing provider in 'bulk' and selling to the community at a lower-than-market-rate
- allowing market forces to take effect and allowing the community to make its own choices.

Ubiquitous community access

The third issue to consider with regard to information access is ensuring that all members of the community, should they so desire, can have access to the community network. For the project to claim to be a true community network, all members of the community must be able to have access to the network as required. In order to increase awareness and interest amongst these people, it will be necessary to provide start-up funding to provide the infrastructure to enable access and longer-term funding to increase usage. Part of the process involved will be the use of development workers, who will train and advise with regard to Internet connection and usage.

There are two main categories of people with regard to Internet access:

- organizations and individuals who can afford their own connection
- those members of the community without sufficient funds, to whom the cost of connection must be subsidized.

It is in the interest of the community network that as many people as possible use the system. For example, it is in the interests of the companies providing information for pages that the pages should be accessed by as many people as possible.

Information provision

The issues to be examined in relation to information provision are the ownership and the maintenance of the information.

Going from one extreme to the other, there are three possible scenarios that can be followed:

1   Each individual information provider is responsible for updating its own pages.
2   The system operator will be responsible for updating some pages and some individuals will be responsible for updating their own pages.
3   The system operator will be responsible for maintaining and updating all pages.

Some information will need more regular updating than others. For example, a commercial site might need updating daily or more often, whereas a listing of tourist amenities might only need to be changed on a yearly basis. A system that will allow flexibility for the different types of information contained will be the more desirable.

Community involvement

The structure selected must be geared to the needs of all the community. The sectors of the community that must be catered for are: business, local government, education, the non-profit sector, and individuals/community groups. As can be expected, these groupings will have vastly different expectations and needs. To cater most effectively for these different groups, development workers will be required to work with and for the different sectors. Individuals with a relevant background will be needed to work with the different sectors, on a full or part-time basis.

Project structure for phase 2

A structure such as outlined below is envisaged to manage the project during phase 2:

- project manager – full-time, with overall responsibility for development of the project
- education worker – approximately two days a week, to deal with all the education sectors in the community
- a community worker – approximately two days a week, to liaise with the council, voluntary and non-profit sectors, community groups and individuals
- secretary for office and reception functions.

Plan also to 'buy in' additional technical services as required.

The Morino Institute[1] has this to say about the staffing of a community network:

> The staffing requirement is much more than hiring someone to administer the network. Certainly, network administration is an important responsibility, but it is far less relevant to long-term success than staff to provide community engagement, promotional seminars, fund raising, periodic community needs assessment, education and training, telephone support, and even consulting services.

A **board of directors**, formed from the partners identified in phase one and representative of the community as a whole, should oversee the project and meet at intervals to examine progress and to plan future strategies. This notion of a board overseeing the community network is again in line with the recommendations of the Morino Institute[1] with regard to community involvement in the project – they suggest a board of directors that is

> . . . composed of active, engaged agents of community change – people from diverse backgrounds, with a range of relevant opinions and experiences. Your Boards should be selected to include: those who will connect you to key bases of support; those who can help you raise funding; those who will contribute management know-how; and, most importantly,

those who believe in the potential of community networking and who will work to help sell and engage the people and institutions of the community. The Board should be composed of people who will continually challenge the community network to grow, to develop, and to improve – to question its own status quo.

A **public access point** should be provided to enable individuals who would not otherwise have access to the Internet to be able to connect to the community information network. These terminals should be placed in such locations as libraries and community centres

The provision of training will be a vital part of the project to ensure that the community has the necessary skills to exploit the potentials offered by the community network.

In addition to development workers for the different sectors of the community, funding should be made available to enable groups in the voluntary sector, the education sector and the business sector actually to get connected to the community network.

Project costings

The cost of developing the community network must be looked at in two parts – the initial cost of setting up the business, during phase 2 and the ongoing costs associated with the day-to-day running of the business following the conclusion of phase 2.

Set-up costs

Work package 1: World Wide Web Server

Aim: The establishment of a WWW server.

The project intends to provide a server on which the pages for the community network will be placed. This will mean that space can then be sold to companies or individuals wishing to have a website.

The establishment of the World Wide Web server will include sourcing and purchasing the machine, installation and configuration of World Wide Web Server software.

Tasks:

1   The purchase/ lease of a machine that will be the WWW server:
    This cost includes hardware, software and maintenance for phase 2,
    and is indicative rather than fixed.
2   Establishing Internet connection:
    Decisions taken regarding required bandwidth will affect the cost.
3   Setting up the machine.
4   The physical location of the server:
    There may be an element of rent for space that server physically
    occupies.

Deliverable: WWW server for the project set up and running.
Timescale: Complete three months from start of phase 2.

Work package 2: Set-up of organization

Aim: The establishment of a not-for-profit company.
As previously outlined, it is recommended that the project will be managed by a not-for-profit organization during phase 2, with the aim of
setting up a self-funding organization following this two-year phase.

   The initial organization will be overseen by a committee of representatives from all sectors of the community. There will be a full-time
manager and secretary for the organization, and part-time workers to
develop the voluntary/community sectors and the education sector.

   The project will host the information on its server, but will not act as
an Internet service provider. Members of the community will have the
cost of access to the community network Subsidized where necessary.

Tasks:

1   Employing initial staff
    Full-time costs for two years (cost includes salary, employer's costs
    and administration costs):
    •   project manager
    •   secretary
    Part-time costs.
2   Forming a committee
    Bringing together a group of representatives from the various sec-

tors of the community to form a strategic committee that will meet to guide the longer-term development of the organization. This committee would be served by the project manager.

3   Marketing costs
To include such costs as local advertising, developing public information brochures, stationery (headed paper, business cards, compliments slips), design costs (logo) and mail-shots.

4   Premises
Costs will depend on the choice of location.

5   Office equipment
It is assumed that the premises will provide office furniture as a minimum.
   • office computers
   • printer
   • fax machine.

6   Office running costs
Including telephone charges, postal charges, electricity, photocopying.

Deliverable: The establishment of a self-financing organization to manage the facility following the end of phase 2.
Timescale: Two years from start of phase 2.

Work package 3: The voluntary sector

Aim: To encourage participation and build support from the not-for-profit organizations in the community.

> Every non-profit organization has two primary resources: people and their ideas. What the Internet offers is an easy, immediate, extremely efficient way to connect with people and ideas . . . the Net as a way to network and to communicate with peers is invaluable, and access to various on-line information depositories can drastically reduce time needed for research . .
> One contributor to this thread commented, 'I have a feeling of urgency about the subject of NPOs on the 'Net: that as technology continues to accelerate, we could very easily be left behind if we do not develop our own survival strategies'. . . [2]

These organizations will not have large financial resources, but the information they can provide will be very important for the success of the community network. Pages have already been developed free of charge for some of these organizations. It is hoped to get more organizations involved, from the not-for-profit sector, both in terms of information access and provision.

Tasks:
1 Employment of a voluntary sector development worker:
  - to work two days a week with the various not-for-profit organizations and community groups
  - full-time cost for two years (including salary, 26.5% employer's costs and 25% administration costs).
2 Subsidizing the costs of connection:
  This subsidy will include the cost of connection, a percentage of the communications cost and possibly the provision of modems. The cost of this is expected to be in the region of £500 per organization.

Deliverable: A large proportion of the community groups and not-for-profit sector aware of and using the community network, both in terms of information access and information provision.
Timescale: Two years from start of phase 2.

Work package 4: The education sector

Aim: To encourage participation and build support from all levels of the education sector in the area.

> The student sits at a classroom computer grazing Internet – a global network linking the student with vast databases, innumerable bulletin boards and millions of users. The potential is amazing . . . [3]

This wealth of information is something that all schools should have access to. However access is only part of the challenge: once connected, the staff and students must learn to use the resources available to benefit properly. This will involve someone who has knowledge both of the Internet and of the education system working with those people involved in the education sector in the area. There has to be a major investment in schools, since unless children learn the necessary skills at an early age, they will be disadvantaged compared with those who have learned them.

Tasks:

1   Employment of an education development worker to work one day a week with the various schools and educational establishments, including members of staff, groups who already work with the student to increase awareness and usage levels. The person to be employed should be a practising teacher with experience of the use of Internet in schools. Full-time cost for two years includes salary, 26.5% employer's costs and 25% administration costs.
2   To subsidize the cost of educational establishments becoming connected.

Deliverable: A large proportion of all levels of educational institutions aware of and using the community network, both in terms of information access and information provision.
Timescale: Two years from start of phase 2.

Work package 5: Business usage

Aim: To encourage participation by, and build support from, the business sector.

> If you are not on the Internet you are not going to be around by the end of the decade. What future is there for traditional banking when you can log on, go through some serious security barrier, then manipulate your money on the screen? What future is there for traditional software distribution when you can log on, download some demo software, like it, pay for it with plastic money, then have it downloaded to your PC?[4]

Whether or not the Internet becomes as all important for businesses as the above writer would have us believe, there are already a number of good reasons for companies to consider the Internet for their companies.

Any business with a product or service that has an international appeal can afford to open an international office and initiate an international marketing campaign right from their current location. Your Internet presence can become your brochure, catalogue, price list and/or all-around selling presentation as well as your international site or location. Once on the Internet, your business will have a local office in each destination where a computer is connected into the Internet.[5]

It is important for the success of the community network that as many as possible of an area's business sector become involved in the project. The income received from the business sector will be used in the development of other sectors of the network.

A further reason for the importance of the business sector is their willingness to become information providers, which will determine the amount and type of information that is available for the community to access. There must be information of interest to the community for them to use and reuse the network on an ongoing basis.

Tasks: Subsidizing the consultancy costs for a business to be connected to the network. It is not intended to employ a technical consultant on a full-time basis as it is felt that it would be more effective to hire such services as required. The subsidy would cover part of the consultancy costs of setting up the Internet connection.
Deliverable: A large proportion of the local business sector aware of and using the community network, both in terms of information access and information provision.
Timescale: Two years from start of phase 2.

Work package 6: Individual access

Aim: To ensure that all individual members of the community that wish to can have access to the community network.

For a community network to be successful it must involve all of the sectors of the community and as many of the individuals in the community as well.

The community network needs to represent the interest of the community it serves . . . The community networking programs that will succeed in the long run will be those that have maintained a focus on the multiplicity of needs in the community and have effectively engaged the full spectrum of their neighbors.[6]

Therefore, all members of the community, whether or not they have a computer at home, must have the opportunity to access the network. This will be achieved by the installation of a number of public access points in locations to which the community has access such as libraries and community centres.

> We believe it is imperative that anyone who cannot link themselves into the information society at home should be able to go into their public library – or perhaps in some areas their village hall – and do it there. Some local authorities are already well advanced in this, and many are already choosing to make use of information technology in their libraries and public buildings.[7]

Commenting on a project in Solihull, Batt[8] noted that

> The library has CD-ROM, computer assisted learning, and the Internet, all for direct public access. The project is still in progress and results are, therefore, not yet available, but it is already evident that community demand for the services, including the Internet, far outstrip the resources that can be provided.

Tasks: To provide public access points, including the purchase cost of equipment, set-up charges, annual connection charges and a proportion of telephone costs. The ongoing costs will be met for the period of one year. Initially ten sites could be set up in the surrounding areas.
Deliverable: A high proportion of the community using the network both for information access and information provision.
Timescale: Two years from start of phase 2.

Work package 7: Training and awareness raising

Aim: To ensure that the community is aware of the community network and receives training to enable them to use the community network and broader sources of electronic information (FTP, electronic mail, news groups and so forth).

Many of the potential users in the community will have used computers before and some will have used the Internet, but more importantly, in training terms, are those members of the community that have perhaps never used a computer in their life.

> For many would-be users, a blank computer screen is as formidable a barrier as a deadbolt. Certainly computer interfaces have improved markedly in the past few years, especially for Internet use, but we have inched up to 1, perhaps 2, on a scale of 1 to 10. It is still a chore for many people and a barrier to many.[6]

Without the provision of training, many members of the community will neither know how to, nor dare try to, use the community network, and the community network will have failed in its aims and objectives by excluding them.

Tasks:
1   Training days
    These would be aimed at a specific group of people and would be designed around their specific needs. Each training day would cater for approximately 20 people and there would be 24 such days during phase 2.
2   Development meetings
    These would be aimed at larger groups and designed as introductory sessions to explain and introduce the notion of the community network, and there would be 24 such meetings during phase 2.

Deliverable: It is expected that two types of people would emerge from the training process – namely, those who had learned to use the network for themselves, and also those who could train others to use the network.

Timescale: Two years from start of phase 2.

Ongoing costs following the completion of phase 2

- premises – rent
- personnel
  - — manager (full-time)
  - — secretary (full-time)
- systems maintenance (hardware and software)
- cost of Internet connection
- office costs
- marketing costs

Future development

Following the end of phase 2, ownership of the project will revert back entirely to the community. Steps must be taken during these two years to ensure that all the necessary skills are in place successfully to manage the project in the long term.

Some further ideas for the development of the project in the longer term could involve an increase in the range of information covered – for example, transport timetables, local news, classified section, IRC channel or newsgroups. The more the community uses and benefits from their own and other networks, the more knowledgeable they will become as to the types of information they would like to see featured on their network.

The need for training and education will have to be met on an ongoing basis, training and educating new users and furthering the knowledge and abilities of current users. There is still a great need for people to learn information skills: how to retrieve and evaluate information.

References

1   The Morino Institute, *Doors of opportunity for local communities*, Reston, VA, 1995. Available at
    <http://www.cais.com/morino/htdocs/pandintr.htm>.
2   SOC.ORG.NONPROFIT and USNONPROFIT-L, Information for non-profits, *Frequently asked questions 1994–1995*. Available at
    <http://www.eskimo.com/~pbarber/npo-faq-pl l.html>
3   McKenzie, J, *Grazing the Net: Raising a generation of free range students –*

part one, 1994. Available at
<http://www.pacificrim.net/~mckenzie/grazingl.html>

4   Barker, J, *Inside multimedia*, 30 November 1994, 30. Quoted in Edupage 21, February 1995, service by Educom. Washington, DC. Available at <http://www.educom.edu(edupage.old/edupage.95/edupage-02.21.95>

5   DesignNet Productions, Inc, *Benefits of an electronic presentation*. Available at <http://www.dynapro.com/dynamic/electronic.presentation.html>

6   Morino, M, *Assessment and evolution of community networking* (paper presented at the 'Ties that Bind' Apple Computer/Morino Institute Conference 'On building community computing networks', 5 May, 1994, Apple Computer, Cupertino, CA, 1994. Available at <http://www.cais.com/morino/htdocs/ties94sp.htm>

7   British Labour Party, *Communicating Britain's future: Labour's information superhighway policy*, 1997. Available at <http://www.poptel.org.uk/labour-party/policy/infohighway/index.html>

8   Batt, C, *The library of the future: public libraries and the Internet* (paper delivered at the 61st IFLA General Conference – 20–25August,1995). Available at <http://www.nlc-bnc.ca/ifla/conf/ifla6l/61-batc.htm>

4

Better communities through better information
Project CIRCE and community information

Helen Leech

Introduction

Networking is a key word in public libraries at the moment. Reports
about the public library sector over the past ten years have been calling
for it. New technologies are not just available for it, but are making it
rosily attractive. The leading organizations in the sector have been
involved in the report *New Library: The people's network*,[1] which has produced an exciting vision of the public library of the future, and have followed it up with *Building the New Library*,[2] which has put together
practical proposals for doing so. And the government has not only given
approval to digital information, but is also putting money behind it.

Things have not looked so promising for the public library world for
a long time. A number of projects have sprung up, putting together
structures for networking, and one of them is the CIRCE project, a
British Library[3]-funded project researching the possibilities of networking community information. It is managed by Gloucestershire
Libraries,[4] Croydon Libraries,[5] UKOLN[6] (the UK Office for Library
and Information Networking), and EARL[7] (the consortium of public
library authorities).

Public libraries provide community information as one of their core
services. They have long recognized that healthy communities depend
on the free flow of accurate information. They pull together lists of
local doctors, contact details for councillors, leaflets about housing
benefit, booklets of local train and bus times, minutes of council meet-

ings, details of where to go for help on any subject, annual reports for local organizations, lists of clubs – any kind of information you might need for solving practical day-to-day problems, any kind of information you might need for finding out what's going on in your community. In the 1980s, many libraries saw the advantages of converting this information into electronic form, and many saw the advent of Teletext, Viewdata and Prestel as the solution to making community information universally available. That vision never really achieved its full potential, but now technology is available which is making the vision clearer than ever.

The Internet

The Internet is already a rich community information resource, and many organizations are realizing the benefits of putting their information on it. Amongst them, public libraries are moving rapidly to make their databases available. About 30 authorities in the UK[8] now have community information systems which are accessible via the Internet, and more are using new technologies to make information available via local networks, intranets, one-stop-shops, kiosks and cable television channels. It is becoming increasingly clear that the Internet offers the public library world an unprecedented medium both for accessing information sources and for making their own information available to the public. Public libraries are using the Internet to make their files available outside their buildings and outside their opening hours, and as Internet access increases, more and more people are finding the information they need right there on their desktop.

Project CIRCE

Project CIRCE is a research project looking at the issues to do with using Internet or other new technologies to network community information. Think of the benefits of being able to tap into details of local childminders, training courses, jobs, tax tables, theatre performances, council services or school prospectuses, without having to phone around – without even having to explore numerous websites. The vision behind CIRCE is the creation of a system where information is brought together from distributed databases in as user-friendly a way as possible.

What level of networking is feasible?

This is a question which library authorities will have to answer them-selves, if they decide to participate in networking community informa-tion. From a technical viewpoint, the technology is already available and being used. Subject gateways such as ADAM[9] and OMNI[10] bring together resources on particular subjects from across the Web in a very effective way; alternatively, COPAC[11] shows how information can be harvested from distributed databases and presented to the end user.

The technology is there, but libraries will have to decide how to use it. To test the waters, CIRCE held a workshop in mid-January 1999, attended by representatives from a quarter of all the library authorities in the UK. They were shown the CIRCE research, and asked how they would like to see a networked service develop. The messages from the various discussions were plain: libraries can clearly see the advantages of networking information, and feel the time is right – indeed, they feel that they need to seize the moment. However, there is a recognized lack of uniformity of provision across the library sector, and a clear call for developing common 'standards', not only to enable exchange of information between authorities but also for the benefit of those authorities who are only just setting out on the electronic superhigh-way. The workshop has given clear direction to the last months of the CIRCE project, which is now going on to identify core materials, stan-dards, management possibilities and funding sources, while developing a technical solution to networking.

Library authorities

What will library authorities have to do to make their community information systems networkable? Many authorities already have well-established electronic community information systems, which they have had for years. As mentioned above, Teletext and Viewdata were used very successfully in many libraries, and still are in 15% of them, although increasingly the information is being converted to web pages.

Some 23% of library authorities use their library management systems
to offer information, so that it can be made available on the same terminals as they use for their OPACs. Some 23% are using databases,
sometimes just for staff use, but mainly offered for public use on stand-
alone PCs, kiosks in community places, or networks across a city or
area. And 22% are using the Internet to provide information, sometimes consisting of tens of thousands of records.[12]

Because these services are well established – and are very successful
– CIRCE is reluctant to suggest that authorities will have to change
their working practices or their information structures. Consequently
the main aim of the project is to look at the possibility of finding a piece
of 'middleware' which is capable of harvesting information from existing databases and html pages.

At the same time, however, 25% of library authorities are still using
paper-based systems to deliver their community information. They are
authorities who perhaps have not had the political will, or the demand
from their communities, or the resources, to venture into electronic
information. Within this group, there is a great deal of movement, with
many having specific plans to provide information via the Internet.
Because they are just starting out, they are casting around for information and for examples of best practice, and if, at this stage, they can
implement common standards, then the idea of networking in the
future becomes more practicable.

Features of community information networks

What kind of features will networked community information have to
have? Community information consists of two types of information:[13]
firstly, *survival* information. A member of the public has a particular
need, and wants to know where to go to satisfy that need. For example,
somebody who has just been told they have cancer may be looking for
support groups; somebody who has just retired may be looking for a
day-time class to join; somebody who has a problem with a party wall
may be looking for a solicitor, or a place to go for advice.

The second type of community information is *citizen action* information, which allows people to participate in local processes. For example,
if the council is planning a local by-pass around the town, then resi-

dents might be looking for plans of the by-pass, minutes from the Highways Committee of the Council, and statistics about road traffic through the town.

As can be seen, people are looking for information about a particular subject or about a particular area, and often the two combined. This raises certain issues.

Metadata systems

To start with, in order to harvest information from existing databases, the software doing the harvesting has to recognize the elements of the record it is taking: what the subject is, where the contact details are, what the title is. This implies a certain degree of cataloguing, which is already taking place in public library databases. However, the cataloguing systems being used are very idiosyncratic, usually developed in-house. This should not present insurmountable problems where library authorities have well-developed systems, since they will just have to 'map' the elements they are using to the elements used by the middleware. Where libraries are just starting along this route, however, they may do well to consider using common cataloguing systems, known in the Internet world as *metadata*.

The good thing about the metadata systems being developed is that they offer the potential for all kinds of organizations to exchange information, and to make their information more easily accessible to the public. The three metadata systems which look most promising are: Dublin Core,[14] GILS (Government Information Locator Service),[15] and USMARC Format for Community Information.[16] Many organizations are working on these, and if they become industry standards, then anybody who uses them would find their information compatible with information from many other organizations. For example, if we were to use Dublin Core to catalogue a record about a local production of Othello, then potentially anybody searching for 'Othello' would find our record, plus printed copies of the play, plus video clips from great performances, plus sound clips from the opera.

The bad thing about these metadata systems is that they are very experimental, few organizations are using them yet, and with the exception of USMARC they are not ideal for cataloguing community information. However, we should bear in mind that it could be possible to adapt one or more of the schemes for our own purposes.

Leading on from the issue of cataloguing is that of subject indexing. Libraries' community information systems are based very strongly on subject searching, but the subjects differ from authority to authority, and no national thesauri exist (with the possible exception of Hasset,[17] which was created for social researchers). For example, people using the library in a rural area will have different information needs from those living in an urban area, and the information their libraries offer will reflect this. Librarians typically build up subject thesauri over time, which they use in indexing the records they add to their databases, but these thesauri are seldom shared between authorities.

Thesauri may not be necessary, depending on what we decide we want from our future network. We could decide to use freetext searching, which is very well understood thanks to the Internet's many search engines, and which if used by an experienced searcher produces good results. However, if we want extremely precise searches, freetext searches are not adequate. How precise do we want to get?

Location indexing

And what about location indexing, which presents a different set of problems? Librarians approach the issue in a multitude of ways. In small authorities, no location indexing is used. If your database consists of a handful of records spread over an area a few miles wide, then there is no need to index by location. The other bigger authorities use postcodes, post towns, electoral wards, home-grown area lists, lists provided by the local authority, lists of local authority areas, lists of towns and villages, and in a couple of cases they use maps. This is a significant problem. If we want to supply information across the country, then we are going to have to give people consistent means to search for that information. There are ways of approaching this, including using external thesauri such as that produced by the Ordnance Survey,[18] or a mapping system such as that provided by Multimap.[19]

Users

Other features of the central harvesting software will have to be agreed. Two of the most probable, used by many library authorities, are those of *user group* and *user need*. The issue of grouping information by the type of person who needs it is contentious, and although some authorities find it useful if not essential, others don't need it. User groups usually include ethnic groups, but can also cover people with disabilities, particular age groupings, and groups by sexuality.

The idea of grouping information by *user need* is a more recent concept, and many organizations are starting to group information by *life episode* rather than by which council department provided it (which was a singularly unhelpful system). The idea behind life episodes is that people experience similar needs at intervals throughout their lives, such as starting school, finding work, getting married, buying a house, having a child, retiring — each of which involves different community information needs.

The core of the CIRCE concept, then, is to find a way of harvesting information from existing, distributed, diverse systems. But there are other, side issues which bear considering.

Who is the system intended for?

The user interface, the 'front end', needs to be tailored accordingly. For the 'man in the street' it has to be user-friendly. For the librarian, it has to offer advanced search options. For those with visual impairments, it has to meet the RNIB's requirements.[20] For ethnic groups, it could be presented in other languages.

Information could be packaged to meet particular needs — for example, if a health authority wanted information on health and related matters, these could be drawn together from the resources of a number of libraries and packaged on disc, or across a network, or via the Internet, or on paper. There are a couple of projects being run by public libraries which target particular information to particular user communities, such as social workers, health workers or sports coordinators; a national network would offer them the opportunity to do this on a larger scale.

Would the system be visible or invisible? In other words, would the person sitting in front of a terminal realize that the information he or she was accessing was coming from a number of different authorities? This is an issue for some authorities, who have to prove to their masters that they are providing services first and primarily to their own communities, and who may have issues around the ownership of the information.

What about the human factor?

Acting as information intermediaries, and creating centres of social interaction, is one of the great unsung roles of the public librarian. There is a danger that authorities, carried away by the potential and excitement of new technologies (and the potential savings), will assume that unmanned databases can replace manned enquiry services. But the role of the librarian extends far beyond the simple provision of information, and people who have difficulty accessing information for one reason or another are likely to be left worse off than ever if the human intermediary is removed – and they are the people who need the information most. Readers interested in this issue may want to see the reports produced by the project The Social Impact of Public Libraries.[21]

'Ask a Librarian'

Certain projects already exist which are addressing this. 'Ask a Librarian'[22] is an Internet enquiry service managed by EARL, the consortium of public libraries, which takes e-mail enquiries from anybody who cares to ask, and routes them to one of approximately 40 participating library authorities to provide an answer. The Regional Information Service[23] does the same for enquiries about the North of England, routing enquiries to its 13 member library authorities. Many individual library authorities field enquiries via their web pages. Should a community information network include a central, manned enquiry point?

What kind of network?

And, finally, what kind of network are we discussing? Should it be a central database, a collection of regional solutions, a subject gateway, a web ring, a search engine, or something completely new? At the time of writing, we are in the process of finding a technical consultant whose job it will be to lay out the technical solutions. Once we know what is feasible, CIRCE will be better prepared to consult the library world to find out how it sees networked community information progressing.

This chapter has presented a number of issues, which could be seen as barriers to networking community information. They are not barriers; they are challenges. No other organization is so well placed to bring together information about people and communities. No other professionals have a combination of skills which librarians have, and which makes them ideally suited to playing a key role in the government's agendas of promoting lifelong learning and preventing social exclusion. Public libraries have long been information hubs for the communities they serve, and the fact that these hubs are rapidly becoming electronic will only ensure better services. If public libraries come together to network community information, then the result will be a wider, faster flow of information – and better communities.

For more information about the project, contact Helen Leech, CIRCE Project Officer, Gloucestershire Library HQ, Quayside House, Gloucester, GL4 4DQ, UK; tel: +44 (0) 1452 425361; e-mail: hleech@gloscc.gov.uk. There are detailed web pages about the project at <http://www.gloscc.gov.uk/circe/>.

References

1   <http://www.ukoln.ac.uk/services/lic/newlibrary/>
2   <http://www.lic.gov.uk/publications/building.html>
3   <http://www.bl.uk/services/ric/>
4   <http://www.gloscc.gov.uk>
5   <http://www.croydon.gov.uk/>
6   <http://www.ukoln.ac.uk>
7   <http://www.earl.org.uk/index.html>
8   Details of these authorities can be found at
    <http://www.gloscc.gov.uk/circe/ciproj.htm>
9   <http://www.adam.ac.uk>
10 <http://www.omni.ac.uk>
11 <http://cs6400.mcc.ac.uk/copac/>

12 Figures are taken from a survey of 113 library authorities carried out by
    CIRCE early in 1997. There are 208 authorities in the UK in total.
13 This definition is based on the work of Joseph C Donohue of the Food
    and Drug Administration in Washington DC, USA, quoted in Bunch,
    A, *More than just books*, Branch and Mobile Libraries Group of the
    Library Association, 1979, p.3.
14 <http://purl.oclc.org.dc/>
15 <http://www.ukoln.ac.uk/metadata/cld/study/collection/gils/>
16 <http://lcweb.loc.gov/marc/community/eccihome.html>
17 <http://dawww.essex.ac.uk/projects/thesaurus.html>
18 More details available at
    <http:www.ordsvy.gov.uk/literatu/infopapr/1997/pap1397.html>
19 <http://uk.multimap.com/>
20 <http://www.rnib.org.uk/wedo/research/hints.htm>
21   For details, contact Kevin Harris of the Community Development
    Foundation at kevin@cdf.org.uk
22   <http://www.earl.org.uk/ask/index/html>
23   <http://www.ris.niaa.org.uk>

5
The technologies available

GRAHAM BAGSHAW

Introduction

Most community information networks (CINs) that are being built at present, and that will be built in the foreseeable future, will be based on the Internet for their information and communications facilities. Also, most will be accessed using IBM-compatible PCs operating Microsoft Windows 95/98, Windows NT and their successors. Although this does not represent the complete picture, this chapter is based on these two assumptions.

It is a cliché to say that the pace of technology change is forever increasing. But this must be particularly true of information communications technology (ICT) on which CINs are based. For example, five years ago only a small minority of people in UK communities had even heard of the Internet or the World Wide Web. In one respect this review can therefore only be a snapshot of the technologies available in the early part of 1999. However, the technological approaches which are currently being used do have some degree of stability. For example, while new facilities are being added to Web browsers almost every day, the Web has become a standard technology for addressing the informational requirements of CINs. Building community information networks is a slow and expensive process, and people are slow to change and to throw away what has been hard to build and learn. CINs will therefore not succeed unless there is a good degree of stability, and unless technological change can be accommodated strategically into their development.

Only two or three years ago, accessing and using the Internet was not a straightforward business, but, happily, this has now changed – the explosion in its usage reflects this. The use of graphical user interfaces (eg those based on Microsoft Windows) and the development of the Web have been the main factors that have influenced this change. So, for the users of community networks, things are now relatively straightforward. However, setting up and managing the technology needed for building and running a CIN requires a greater understanding of the underlying issues and potential pitfalls. This chapter is intended to provide guidance in these areas.

Knowing what the Internet can offer

So, if you're starting from scratch, having learned to surf the Web and to send e-mail, the next thing to do is to get a better feel for the Internet and what it can offer – by doing a bit of reading. There is an ever-increasing number of texts about the Internet on the shelves of most bookshops, and browsing will fairly easily help to identify those which will suit the reader's needs. One book which has existed in one form or another for several years, and which was for a long time regarded by many as the 'Internet's Bible', is *The whole Internet* by Ed Krol.[1] The latest version, although published in 1995, still gives a thorough introduction to the Internet, is easy to read, entertaining, and can be read selectively.

The Internet will provide facilities for at least two of the basic electronic functions of a CIN:

- e-mail and e-mailing lists – to address the communications requirement
- the Web – to address the information requirement.

In planning, designing, and setting up a CIN, the following technological issues need to be considered:

- how to provide users with access to the Internet
- how to organize communications using e-mail
- how to set up and maintain a presence on the World Wide Web.

These and some other issues are addressed in the remainder of the chapter.

Some general issues

Fundamental to the network will be access to the Internet, e-mail and server space for the website. Note that this need not be provided by a single Internet service provider (ISP) – one might choose one ISP to provide access to the Internet and to handle the e-mail, and another to host the website. While this can be a little less straightforward, it can give greater flexibility, eg for Web presence one might rent a virtual Web server from a company which specializes in this part of the business.

Some of the issues that need to be resolved can be quite complex and tricky – the whole scenario consists of a collection of various bits and pieces that need to be made to fit comfortably together. ISPs will almost invariably be ready to help with this, but they have a different point of view from the user, and a vested interest. For instance, they are unlikely to suggest that one might be better using another company's facilities for part of the job. Therefore, depending on their level of knowledge and experience, designers and builders of networks might find it necessary first to seek independent advice from a technical specialist.

For many reasons, it is desirable for a CIN to register an Internet domain name, for example, <CINname.org.uk> or <CINname.org>, where 'CINname' mnemonically identifies the network or project. For example, the Handsworth network has the domain name <handsworth.org.uk>. Bear in mind that such names are unique and are generally assigned on a 'first come first served' basis. The organization which registers the domain on behalf of the CIN will usually make a one-off charge, and there is also likely to be an annual maintenance charge, which may, or may not, include the charge levied by the registration authority (in the UK this is Nominet). These domain costs might be identified separately, or bundled with, say, the annual charge for Web space.

Registration of a domain name can be made through an ISP, or via online services using the Web. Whilst the latter can sometimes appear to be offering a bargain, it is as well to remember that a domain name is of little use by itself: it needs to be integrated with other services (such as e-mail and Web services) and the initial saving made by registering a name with a cheap online service can result in frustrating delays, and possibly further costs, further down the line.

The domain name is used both for the website address (formally called the Uniform Resource Locator, or URL), eg <http://www.handsworth.org.uk>, and for e-mail addresses, eg <admin@handsworth.org.uk>. Apart from its mnemonic appeal, a well-chosen domain name can result in a shorter URL, which usually means that the end-user will find it less of a chore to type. In addition, a major benefit is the provision of independence. For example, a change of ISP can be made without the need to change Web and e-mail addresses on any printed stationery, in users' records and so on. However, moving a domain from one ISP to another can be problematical. For example, an ISP who is losing the business might not give the related work a high priority!

For CINs, '.org' domains are usually appropriate – these are intended to indicate the non-profit status of the organization bearing the name. Either <CINname.org.uk> or <CINname.org> (the international variety) can be registered, but the <CINname.org.uk> version is usually preferred for CINs in the UK – if an organization is geographically localized, then it makes sense to choose a name which helps to portray this.

Access to the Internet

For individual users of the CIN, providing access involves little more than arranging an Internet connection from a PC using a modem and a phone line. However, the CIN organization might also need to provide access from local area networks (LANs) – for example, at public access points and in training centres, where several workstation computers (say up to about 20), need to connect to the Internet (and other facilities) simultaneously.

LANs can be of the 'peer-to-peer' type, where all the computers run the same operating system (eg Windows 95) and all have the same status; or one computer can be designated as a *file server* and will typically run an operating system (called a *network operating system*) that is different from the one on the remainder of the computers (the *workstations*). The second option has the advantages of higher resilience and security, but is more expensive and requires additional skills to maintain. There are two prominent network operating systems: Novell Netware and Microsoft Windows NT. Netware is more mature and is highly developed. NT is newer, has a workstation counterpart and has similarities with Windows 95/98, which might mean that there will be less learning involved. However, both are quite capable of doing the kind of job needed for LANs associated with CINs.

It is then usually necessary to connect the whole LAN to the Internet, so that, at the very least: (a) all (or selected) workstations can access the Web simultaneously, and (b) e-mail can be exchanged with the Internet as well as locally.

There are several ways of achieving such a connection, and the market will be confusing for the newcomer. The method that we recommend for this kind of environment is what we term an 'Internet access gateway' which provides the following facilities:

- concurrent Internet access for up to about 50 workstations, using only one ISP access account
- access to all types of Internet facility
- a 'firewall' capability so that external users of the Internet cannot access the LAN from outside
- optional control of use of Internet access – one might, for example, wish to control the usage of Internet relay chat (IRC)
- optional monitoring of Internet access – who accesses what, when, and for how long
- monitoring of line usage – so that one can see, for example, how line bandwidth is being utilized
- for an Integrated Service Digital Network (ISDN) line, the ability to use on-demand multilink PPP (see below).

Such gateways can connect to the ISP using a dial-up connection, an ISDN line, or a leased line. Of these, the ISDN option is likely to be the most attractive in that it will support sufficient numbers of concurrent users at a reasonable cost. The appropriate kind of ISDN service is called Basic Rate Interface (BRI), which consists of two channels, each of which provides a data-transfer rate of 64 kb/s – an example is BT's ISDN-2 service. The two channels can be combined to provide a 128-kb/s service – this is known as 'multilink PPP' (MP), which is sometimes also referred to as 'channel bonding'. Note that, for MP to work, it must also be supported by the chosen ISP, and an additional charge will usually be involved. The Internet access gateway should be capable of using the two channels together using MP 'on demand' – eg the second channel will only be brought into service when the LAN Internet activity warrants it.

While ISDN provides much faster connect times and data rates than an ordinary dial-up phone line, the cost is considerably higher. Although the call rates *for each channel* are exactly the same as for a phone line, the rental charges per channel can be considerably higher – typically about twice as much. Also, because of the ease, speed and quietness of the call-setup process, large bills can be built up inadvertently. Worse than this, there are several known circumstances in which spurious ISDN calls can be set up by activities on the LAN which have little or nothing to do with Internet access. So the message is that ISDN is impressive, provides the required facilities, but needs to be carefully configured and treated with vigilance.

For smaller organizations, a viable alternative to ISDN might entail using a modem connection over a normal telephone line: modern so-called '56K' V.90 modems can provide connection speeds of around 40–50 kb/s. However, it is essential to ensure that the ISP chosen to provide the dial-up service supports the V.90 protocol.

Typically, the larger proportion of the call charges (whether dial-up or ISDN) will result from Web access, and e-mail will be responsible for only a small proportion. This is because using the Web is essentially an interactive process, whereas with e-mail only occasional Internet connections are needed (see below).

Communications using e-mail

E-mail is a fundamental ingredient for a CIN in that it provides an efficient and popular means of communication between individuals and groups. In general, individual users of the CIN in the community will have e-mail addresses which are assigned by their ISP, but the organizing group will often wish to have addresses which are associated with the domain name, eg <admin@CINname.org.uk>, <fred@CINname.org.uk>, and so on. The CIN's ISP can arrange for all e-mail to the domain to be automatically forwarded to the CIN's Internet account (this is called a domain mailbox). It is then up to the CIN to arrange for the mail to be distributed to individual users' mailboxes. Where a LAN is involved, this is normally achieved by using a local e-mail system on the LAN, and an 'e-mail gateway' which not only sends out local mail to the Internet as needed, but also collects mail for the domain from the Internet and distributes it locally, on a scheduled basis – say every hour or two. In cases where a LAN is not involved, and users of the domain make use of different ISPs for Internet access, arrangements can be made accordingly to forward mail which is sent to the domain. Or other arrangements can be made, such as providing Post Office Protocol Version 3 (POP3) mailboxes on the domain, which allow for e-mail delivery to be entirely independent of the access provider.

Communications between groups on a CIN is often achieved using mailing lists on computers called 'list servers' which are connected to the Internet. Other techniques exist on the Internet – in particular, Usenet newsgroups and Web conferencing techniques – but these can be more difficult to set up, and are generally less easy for newcomers to come to grips with.

Mailing lists on list servers are basically the same as the distribution lists that local e-mail systems provide: ie a message sent to the list is consequently sent out to all members of the list. The fundamental difference between the two is that lists on list servers can be accessed from the Internet. They are also more sophisticated in that

- lists can be public or private
- for public lists, people can join and leave a list by sending an e-mail message to the list server
- lists can be unmoderated or moderated – for moderated lists, all messages sent to the list have to be approved by the moderator (a person) before being sent out to the members of the list.

To set up mailing lists, one must have access to a list server. If a 'virtual Web server' is rented for the website, such a facility might be provided as part of the service. Some e-mail gateways (see above) have inbuilt list servers, in which case the facility can be set up and managed locally. Also, there are a number of free Web-based list server services (they are supported by advertising).

The Web presence

A CIN will invariably have a website to address its informational function. This will be different from a typical site on the Web because its primary function will not be to market and sell things, but to provide a valuable source of information for the community. Also, it will be accessed from a wide range of browsers, using a wide range of computers and modem devices which are typically not of the latest technology. It should therefore

- have a clean, tidy, and businesslike appearance
- have a consistent appearance across the pages which make up the site
- be easy to navigate
- be kept up-to-date
- be efficient, and quick to display
- be viewable from a wide range of computer configurations.

Some of these points are a matter of common sense and organization. We will comment only the last two of these, as the technology has a bearing.

Speed of display has fundamentally to do with the size of image files – the size in bytes, that is. To put this in perspective, consider a user connected to the Internet by a 14.4 kilobyte-per-second (kb/s) modem (way below the latest speeds, but some CIN users will have these). Even if there is no delay on the Web server and the intervening Internet, a 20-kilobyte image (relatively small) could take up to 20 seconds to be displayed. So the message is: avoid crowding Web sites with large images. In general, the larger the physical size of the image, the more space in bytes of storage it will take up and the longer it will take to download from the Web server to a user's Web browser. At the same time, the greater the definition of the image, the larger it will be. So often it can be a trade-off between on the one hand impact and quality, and on the other speed of download. Also, in the interests of image size and quality, the most appropriate image format should be chosen. Two formats are commonly understood by Web browsers and are known as:

- Graphical Interchange Format (GIF)
- Joint Photographic Expert Group (JPEG).

GIF is better for simpler images (eg line drawings) and JPEG is better for photographs. Most IT graphics and photographic packages will be able to generate both formats.

When designing a website, it is impossible to know how the site will be viewed – eg which browser, what monitor screen definition, or even which colour resolution will be used? For CIN users there will be a wide range of such things, and an important principle is to try to make sure that the website is viewable by as large a number of users as possible. Here are some suggestions on how to achieve this:

1   Keep things simple: remember that simplicity and elegance can go hand in hand.
2   Stick to published standards of HyperText Markup Language (HTML). There are programs and services available via the Internet that will check this for you.
3   Don't use frames.
4   Don't use Java or JavaScript.
5   Test your site with a range of browsers – at least a range of versions of Netscape Navigator and Internet Explorer.
6   Test your site with a range of screen resolutions.
7   Put a note on the home page stating what you consider to be the minimum requirements to view the site well – for example: 'Please note that to view these pages properly you need a browser with the capabilities of at least Netscape Navigator 2.0 or Microsoft Internet Explorer 3.0, and a 800x600 display with a resolution of at least 256 colours'.

This advice might seem rather dull to the enthusiast, but to make use of smart facilities such as are only provided by the latest version of a particular browser will militate against the principle of wide availability.

How does one develop a website? There is a large range of tools available, some of which are provided free on magazine cover discs and from the Internet. websites are built using the HyperText Markup Language (HTML). It looks more complicated than it is. At one extreme, one can use just a simple text editor such as the Windows Notepad, and generate pages using raw HTML. At the other end of the scale, one can use sophisticated WYSIWYG ('what you see is what you get') tools that require no user knowledge of HTML at all. The disadvantage of the simple approach is that it is rather tedious and prone to error (bear in mind that browsers do not report errors – they just do what they think you have asked them to do!). The advantage, however, is that you're in full control – unlike with the WYSIWYG method, where the software tool is in control. The advantage of the WYSIWYG method is that you can produce pages quickly. A significant disadvantage is that, this way, it is impossible to be sure that what users see on their screens will be the same as the layout that you see on your development screen.

People who embark on the road of Web page design usually try various tools, and eventually home in on one which suits them best. Often this is somewhere in the middle between the two extremes that have been described. We recommend, however, that, even if one of the more sophisticated tools is used, potential website developers should acquire some basic training in the use of HTML. This gives a better feel for the environment, engenders more confidence, and gives the developer more scope in making use of subtle techniques. There are many books on the shelves of bookshops that provided coaching in the use of HTML.

What are the mechanics of developing and mounting a website? The website can be developed locally on any reasonable PC using the tools discussed above. Pages in development are simply held in a suitable folder/directory on the hard disk drive. When the site is sufficiently developed for public view, it can be transferred ('uploaded') to space on a Web server using a File Transfer Protocol (FTP) program. Because the website has to be available at all times on the Internet, the only real option for Web space is to rent it from an ISP or a specialist Web provider company. It is convenient to do this through the ISP that pro-

vides the Internet connectivity, but, depending on specific requirements, it can be better to rent a 'virtual Web server' from a specialist
provider. The advantage of this it that it gives more control and flexibility (it is almost as good as having a Web server sitting in one's own
office). The disadvantage is that it needs more skills to manage it.

The website will never be finished. For success, it will need to be
frequently and regularly maintained and enhanced. Bearing in mind
that more than one person is likely to be involved in this, efforts need
to be carefully managed and coordinated.

The site will be made known to the world by quoting the URL in
community publications, via hypertext links from other community
sites etc, and through search engines. Search engines are not as important to a CIN site as to a commercial site. The subject of search engines
is a fairly large and messy one, and there is insufficient space here to go
into any detail. However, the following points should be noted:

1   Different search engines use different techniques for indexing the
    words held in website; there are few standards. But it is worth look-
    ing for and studying descriptions of these techniques, so as to max-
    imize the visibility of the site to major engines.
2   Different search engines use different ways of expressing search
    questions; again, there are few standards.
3   Using crafty tricks to try to increase the visibility of a site (eg the
    excessive repetition of key words) is a futile business. Search
    engines are often wise to this sort of thing and will penalize one as
    a result.

The Internet service provider

There are now many ISPs in the UK. Charges range from zero (on the
face of it!), through fixed monthly charges, to those which depend on
the amount of connect time used. For community networks, we recommend the second of these options. Bear in mind also that, as with
most things, a good general rule is that you get what you pay for. Paying
a low price can result in poor accessibility and costly support.

So we would recommend that an ISP is chosen for the CIN which
satisfies the following criteria:

1   Monthly charges are fixed, and unlimited access is permitted.
2   Any Internet application (which conforms to the TCP/IP protocol standards) can be run – for example, any e-mail program, Web browser, newsgroup reader, FTP program etc
3   Multilink PPP is supported.
4   There is no limit on the number of e-mail mailboxes that can be used by the customer – ie 'domain mailboxes' are provided so that one does not have to register or pay for individual e-mail mailbox names.
5   The ISP fares well in league tables provided by Internet magazines, particularly in terms of service availability.

Conclusions

This chapter has attempted to give the architect and builder of a community information network some of the practical technical background, and some tips on how to navigate this. In our experience, such information cannot be found in a single textbook: it has been gathered over a number of years from a variety of sources and experiences.

One of the most important considerations to bear in mind all the time is that CINs are built for the community, and as such should be designed so that they are available to as many people as possible. This has several practical consequences. From a technology point of view, it means that one should always remember that a considerable proportion of users will have dated hardware and software with which to access the network. This need not constrain the effectiveness of the network, but it does mean that the design process needs to take careful thought, and will not be able to use the most recent technological products.

References

1   Krol, E and Ferguson, P, *The whole Internet for Windows 95: User's guide and catalog*, O'Reilly and Associates, 1995.

6

The online life of communities
Nurturing community activity in the information society

KEVIN HARRIS

Introduction

Information and communication are essential ingredients in community life. For people to go about their day-to-day lives, support children, interact with public agencies, get to work and so on, sources of information and channels of communication must be readily and constantly available to them. Where communication is severely constrained, where necessary information is not accessible or social networks do not flourish, people can easily become excluded and their communities can atrophy. If a local community is weak – if the 'conditions of community' are not sustainable because of economic stress for example – it will be unable to support its members in time of need. This makes it more difficult for people who are socially excluded to recover and to become reconnected, should they wish to, to the benefits which society may offer.

The notion of a 'sustainable community' implies that people in a given place are communicating and can be informed. In a healthy community, information will always circulate in an unconstrained way, and it will also pass into and out of that community. A sustainable community is not a self-contained one. It is part of the wider society and depends on equilibrium with that wider society in terms of the economy, the environment, information, culture and so on. We may note that many of the factors of social exclusion are highly vulnerable to disequilibrium in these relationships: for example, where mobility to and from centres of employment or hospitals is constrained by poor transport services, or where local economies are particularly susceptible to national or international fluctuation. A disequilibrium between communities and society may make it difficult for people in one locality to retain any wealth, for example; or it may leave them the victims of negative environmental effects as some of the factors of wealth are transported to other communities across their patch. The point is that all communities, and not just those which show most evidence of deprivation, are subject to forces beyond their control. They depend on interactions with the wider society, and on their ability to import and exploit resources, including information. We should keep in mind also that even affluent communities can exhibit many of the symptoms of social exclusion.

Much of the work of compensating for disequilibrium between a community and the wider society falls to the local social economy. In many deprived neighbourhoods, agencies of various kinds strive to make up for a shortfall or shortcomings in the economic, health, educational, environmental and other systems. The social economy is made up of a wide range of non-profit organizations, but its basis is community activity. Community activity brings to the social economy crucial contributions of mutual aid and support, reduced costs, environmental monitoring and improvement, greater pertinence and efficiency in the delivery of services, and so on.

But it seems difficult to ensure that community activity is confirmed as an essential precondition for social and economic development. Numerous social programmes over the last 30 years have led to a new policy commitment on neighbourhood renewal, and increasing recognition that the forces which work against community activity can often be far too strong for residents, community agencies or authorities to overcome by themselves, without collaboration and a strategic approach. Thus one policy objective might be to promote more coordinated efforts at a local level to bring about communities which are

- more autonomous and self-supporting
- less vulnerable to external forces
- not uneconomic and not liable to drain public money
- able to take advantage of connections with the wider society.

Policy cannot be expected to make all communities equal, but it can and should be used to enhance levels of community activity, in order to establish the kind of equilibrium which will make healthy communities sustainable. Information and communication are essential ingredients in this respect, and in this chapter I will explore some key policy questions on sustainable community activity as the notion of an 'information society' begins to come into focus. Consideration is given to the relationship between community activity and the local communication and information environment, with particular reference to the least-integrated neighbourhoods; and we explore ways in which ICTs might affect this relationship. What matters in this context I suggest, is to understand the relationship between the existing conditions of communication in neighbourhoods, and the potential online life of communities. If we can understand the changes implied, it will help us to identify clearly the role for information and communication, and for community networks, in supporting community activity and social cohesion. This chapter is intended to begin articulating the questions which we need to address if social policy is to promote the use of community networks for neighbourhood renewal.

The notion of an 'information society' encourages us to take a fresh look at patterns of information and communication in communities. These patterns themselves may not be about ICTs, but they will be influenced by the increasing role of ICTs. And while policy on community information may be stimulated by ICTs, it needs to be about the whole context of information and communication at local level.

A historical perspective

The emerging information society can look more convincing considered from a historical perspective which explores the impact of the prevailing print-based knowledge culture.[1] We can make assumptions about local communities in Western Europe before the age of print: that they would have been relatively autonomous economically, for example, and that a comparatively small amount of people's information income would have been imported into the community. Knowledge of life beyond the neighbourhood would largely have depended on travellers (including performers), the clergy and the ruling classes. Most people's day-to-day lives would seldom have involved them in communicating with people they did not know.

Over the past 500 years or so, local communities have generally tended to become economically more dependent on the wider society and the global economy. The context of communication has been transformed by the available technology – first of print, then of mass transport, and more recently of telephony and broadcasting – so that

- a large proportion of our information income is generated by mass media and broadcast to us impersonally
- most people are constrained in contributing to the available store of knowledge because of the economics of publishing and broadcasting
- more and more of our communication is not face to face, and not with people we know.[2]

There is thus a lack of correlation between most of the information which we receive (from the news, soap operas, fashion magazines, football reports, etc) and the issues which might involve or concern us about the neighbourhoods we inhabit. Restoring this community information correlation is a critical challenge for community networks.

The 'conditions of community'

In 1998 the Social Exclusion Unit (SEU) published a major report and innovative strategy on neighbourhood renewal: *Bringing Britain together*.[3] The document raises important questions about different kinds of low income neighbourhood. It focuses principally on urban deprivation, because it is concerned with *concentrations* of poverty; and while the title refers to 'Britain' its action is confined to England. The SEU strategy includes the establishment of 18 'policy action teams' (PATs) including one on 'access to IT'[4] and a long-term programme of coordinated action. A key part of the debate is the distinction between two kinds of 'poor neighbourhood': those where community groups are relatively organized and active, where there is professional intervention and perhaps local involvement in regeneration initiatives; and those neighbourhoods where there is little or no visible community activity, where

any groups that exist are fragile and vulnerable, where people are isolated, and preoccupied with survival and trying to escape, and where
'people who can move out.'[5]

In the former, in spite of the level of deprivation, we can see evidence of the 'conditions of community' – the framework on which
renewal can be based. Without this framework, where communities are
dis-integrated, with high levels of economic and social stress, it is unreal-
istic to expect renewal to take root.

By 'conditions of community' I am referring to those local circumstances which help describe people's quality of life and their associations – their everyday interactions with others in the locality which
influence their sense of well-being and security. This corresponds
closely with the thorough analysis of 'the quality of community life'
carried out in recent years by Barr, Hashagen and Purcell.[6] They identify the following characteristics of the 'building blocks of community
development':

- a learning community
- a fair and just community
- an active and organized community
- an influential community
- a commonwealth (local economic development)
- a caring community
- a green community
- a safe community
- a good place to live (people do not wish to leave)
- a lasting community.[7]

These conditions may be a function of a whole range of influences,
such as opportunities for recreation and leisure, availability of local
shops, awareness of local groups, fear of crime, planning for pedestri-
ans, and so on. They may become apparent in levels of facial recognition and frequency of greeting between residents, in opportunities for
informal interaction in the street, shops or park. If these conditions are
sustainable, we would expect to find people communicating and sharing information on an informal basis wherever opportunities arise.

Information and communication in communities[8]

A coherent, healthy community, then, will have key *conduits* for local information, and these will include individuals who are gatekeepers (for example, they will be active on local committees, on community initiatives, perhaps on the parish council and so on), as well as key 'occasions' such as at the school gates, at the pub, walking the dog, at the bus stop, at the youth club or in the corner shop. Significant information exchanges take place in such contexts and it is critical for local information services that this is recognized. Localities also need an appropriate infrastructure of communication systems such as the local newspaper, consultation meetings and telephone network. But my point here is that neighbourhood networks and gatekeepers are *fundamental* to information flow at local level, and any formal community information and communication initiative needs to take this into account. As the INSINC report[1] argues:

> The nature of community communication is likely to change significantly, and the social relevance of small, informal forums could be realized if community networks take full account of the more subtle aspects of the 'neighbourhood network'.[9]

The quality of community life will also depend on a culture of participation, collaboration, diversity and sharing. This is a key factor in information flow. If diversity is not welcomed, and the notion of collaboration is seen more as threat than opportunity, the conditions of community will be weak.

The flow of information depends on two further features: available skills, and relevant content. The kinds of skill needed might be communication skills, information-handling, and processing skills. A key facet of information society development will be citizens' information capability – a combination of information awareness, ability to access information and skill in exploiting it.[10] The kinds of content called for include information about local groups, information about services, details of local businesses etc.

Table 6.1 offers an outline of the suggested features of a flourishing community information environment.

Table 6.1 *Features of a flourishing community information environment*

culture	of participation, collaboration, information sharing, diversity, local awareness, 'a fair and just community'
available **skills**	communication skills: listening, summarizing etc information-handling skills: writing, researching, multimedia, web-crafting etc. information capability: information awareness, access to information, ability to exploit information etc processing skills: negotiating, lobbying, mediation, facilitation etc
responsible **gatekeepers**	key local activists or professionals who are links between information and its applications
'occasions'	informal social opportunities (eg at school gates, in pubs, youth clubs, resource centres, corner shops, walking dogs, at bus stops etc.
appropriate **infrastructure**	local newspaper or newsletter, telephone network (including public call boxes), council committee meeting structure, libraries, c-nets, forums for articulating needs and views, website, public access points etc. (Above all, somewhere for people to go to meet – an agora)
relevant, accessible **content**	official information and information about services, community information, local history and educational resources, local business details etc

In severely disadvantaged communities, by contrast, people's energies and interests may be almost wholly consumed in keeping themselves going and in trying to escape. Isolation, inertia and secrecy may constitute formidable barriers to the flow of information: personal relationships may be scarce and weak, and creative neighbourhood networks may function poorly if at all. One report notes tellingly that:

> The groups which are likely to be on the receiving end of social intervention are not only threatened by the inadequacy of their material resources but also undermined by the fragility of their personal relationships.[11]

A disintegrated community – where there are relatively few community groups, where people are in conflict with authorities, with employers or with one another, or where many people are isolated, uncommunicative or living in fear – is unlikely to have the vital pulse of information flow through which residents share their experiences and act collectively to express their needs and improve their quality of life.

Information flows and social exclusion

It may be important to keep in mind three characteristics of social exclusion which are related to information flows:

- the habit of non-participation
- the habit of isolation
- perceived lack of opportunity.

Many young people go through family and school life, and perhaps into employment, *not expecting* to be consulted about anything and *not expecting* to be invited to participate. Their contribution to, and involvement in, the local informal information network is constrained from an early age. There is clear potential to address this through the sensitive use of ICTs, with participation in discussion through lists, or experimentation with multimedia, for example. The technology can be made accessible in a non-threatening, non-institutionalized way which encourages the expression of views and the lively discussion of common interests.

Similarly, many people have had little experience of travelling beyond their locality and apparently become anchored, unwilling to travel to the next town in search of training or employment.[12] There is often a perception that this is related to what people describe as a 'tight-knit' community, although that doesn't necessarily follow.

This seems to confirm the need for schools to organize visits and trips, and for support for other initiatives such as youth clubs and sports clubs which enable young people to travel beyond their neighbourhood. The potential for community networks to support this with resource material, and to encourage the development of further links with the wider society and with other countries – cultural, educational, business links and so on – needs wider recognition and support.

There are various manifestations of perceived lack of opportunities –

for example, the common assumption with regard to new technologies that 'it's not for the likes of us.' Perceived lack of opportunity is often likely to be a reflection of inadequate information and cultural stifling. One telling comment is cited in the Communities Online submission to the government's Policy Action Team on Access to IT:

> Looking back, I see the main constraint was not having any perception of opportunity when I was growing up. As a sixteen year old girl, getting pregnant or being a secretary was just what you did. You thought it was the only pathway and choice.[13]

One implication is that there is a need at local level for a broader under-standing of life choices which includes, but is not restricted to, career options. This means more than just the long-needed linking of employment and voluntary activity opportunities, but also perhaps using ICTs to explore possible interests and to test ideas in a non-threatening context. After all, for someone whose life-horizons have always seemed inescapably close, the notion of travelling to a nearby town for training and work can be seen as sufficiently threatening as not to be an option or opportunity at all.

The flow of information in neighbourhoods is influenced by other factors such as the relative social mobility of residents, the variety of employment opportunities within and beyond the neighbourhood, or opportunities for informal communication locally. A key factor may be low levels of educational achievement, for example, which does not encourage the use of formal communication media with the wider world. It is not difficult to see how some people experience combina-tions of deprivation which constrict such communication: in one dis-trict of Edinburgh, for instance, we are told that 'It is virtually unknown for anyone from Pilton to enter tertiary education.' The sta-tistics show that 43% of households in Greater Pilton have no earners[14]

Another factor might be so-called 'unofficial housing policies' where the demography is engineered for political reasons and the rate of immigration is too great for local people to absorb it without strong feelings of disturbance. All too often such changes can contribute to 'postcode discrimination' which serves to confirm the exclusion. When such factors are combined with the economic destabilization of small communities – which may have depended heavily, indeed thrived, on a predominantly oral information culture – a healthy level of information flow is sure to be at risk.

If information flow drops below certain critical levels, the *local information ecology* is vulnerable and 'information stagnation' sets in. Levels of face-recognition drop significantly, people stop receiving information (they may stop sharing it), relatively little information goes out of the locality, and the neighbourhood could begin to atrophy. In such a context, the challenge which ICTs may be able to meet is to help establish and sustain healthy conditions for everyday communication to flourish – the kinds of conditions which are critical to sustain the social economy at local level.

Information in communities is diverse, multi-faceted and dynamic. People in communities tend to have relatively unstructured and unsystematic information environments compared with, say, those working in academic or business organizations. At local level, much of an individual's information income may be coincidental, unauthenticated and informal. Thus a conversation between neighbours which begins with a moan about the mess left by the dustmen becomes a discussion about the survival of the local corner shop or the virtues of traffic-calming schemes, or who's got a surplus of cooking apples and what can you do if the cats are fouling the garden right where your daughter plays? In passing, information may be shared about entitlement to benefit for a single mother working part-time. In such a context, we should note two conditions which are highly significant for social inclusion:

1   People make their own judgments, rightly or wrongly, about the authenticity, accuracy and currency of the information they receive on such occasions, and it is a critical role for our education system to ensure that people are as well equipped as possible to make such judgments. In our day-to-day lives, we receive, pass on, and make impromptu judgments about, all kinds of unauthenticated information, all the time.

2   The availability and accessibility of a local, formal information service, to which the individual can turn as a first point of call to verify or to further explore information received in such a context, is of fundamental importance. Without such a facility being seen as a

natural and uncomplicated place to turn, disempowerment through inadequate information will continue as a key feature of social exclusion.

It is also important to recognize that information shared by people in communities probably does not map neatly onto perceptions of 'need to know'. Certainly people will have their own perceived information needs – 'Who knows a reliable plumber? Who can look after my children on Wednesday afternoons?' – but a high proportion of their information income will be coincidental, partial, unauthenticated and partisan. In such contexts, the notion of information as some kind of 'product' delivered by a 'service' has only limited applicability. It may be that many attempts to run community information services have been relatively unsuccessful because of the difficulty of integrating a formal service with the dynamic informality of the neighbourhood communication networks.

With this in mind, we should note that the availability and accessibility of information for political empowerment assumes a particular importance. As I have suggested, information flow may be stifled in a community for a number of reasons; and if people's information environment is very informal, unstructured and relatively slow, they are increasingly at risk of becoming politically isolated. This has potentially dangerous implications, because the pace of decision-making among authorities – indeed, among all kinds of agency – is increasing as the Internet is exploited more widely. Those who are not connected will struggle to engage with the political process and, as one officer has put it, 'Isn't there a risk that, if they don't communicate using this technology, politically they won't exist?'[15]

Communities of interest and need

Distinctions between geographical communities and communities of need or interest can become a matter of conceptual convenience which masks a more fluid reality. Many people involve themselves with communities of interest at and beyond the local level; and it may be that there is greatest (and least-appreciated) value in the knowledge and experience that people bring into their local context from the wider world. The new technologies will certainly provide opportunities to explore and test this hypothesis. As US community networking pioneer Terry Grunwald[8] recently pointed out, ICTs have a role in helping to link people at local level with communities of interest worldwide.[16]

At the same time, however, we can assume that most people's use of online communication will increase, and that therefore the proportion of interaction which people have with others *beyond their own neighbourhood* is likely to increase. This may not necessarily mean that the amount of time they spend communicating *within* their neighbourhoods will decrease. However, we should reflect on the fact that the time and energy we all have for information handling and transfer – formal or informal – is not limitless. Our attention and interest is not boundless, and as the INSINC[1] Working Party put it, 'There is a limit to the amount of information which people are willing to consume'.[17] If we are spending more time in contact with a community of interest whose members are elsewhere on the planet, logically the amount of time spent sharing news and views with neighbours could well decrease.

What are the implications of this? On the one hand, we can foresee a great richness and diversity of experience being brought into local community life through virtual communities. On the other hand, unless it is carefully nurtured, we may find that community activity could contract in many localities as people put their energies, skills and commitment into their virtual communities. Does this matter? For people in neighbourhoods where the information ecology is fragile, it almost certainly does.

In some respects, this may be little more than an extension of a phenomenon which is readily apparent in some wealthy neighbourhoods, where there is relatively little face recognition because houses have large gates and walls, people seldom walk down their own street, and shop at out-of-town hypermarkets or at stores close to their place of work beyond the neighbourhood, and they spend their leisure time with networks of people from geographically dispersed communities such as professional associations, sports and health clubs and so on. Barry Wellman[9] notes that

Most contemporary western communities do not resemble preindustrial villages for they are socially diverse, sparsely knit and well-connected to the outside world. These are only partial communities which do not command a person's full allegiance. Rather, each person is a limited member of multiple communities such as kinship groups, neighborhoods and friendship circles.[18]

This reminds us that the conditions of local community depend on contact and communication with others, not just on inhabiting a shared space. And the virtual equivalent, as journalist Bill Thompson put it, is that 'being online is not the same as being connected to a 'community of others'.[19]

In localities where people are comparatively wealthy, with or without local community ties, we would expect to find that they had effective *connections* with the wider world which in theory are enhanced through ICTs – political, economic and professional connections, for example. In the least-integrated communities, and in low-income localities where there exist strong community ties and a healthy level of community activity, the challenge is to explain and demonstrate how to build such connections using ICTs, while sustaining and strengthening the conditions of local community. Nurturing the online life of communities depends on the kinds of interaction which support, and realize, local community activity.

Communities and individuals

At this point we should note the importance of another continuum, that between the individual and communities. While any community may have a core of people who are constantly involved in what goes on and are stimulating change, many more people drift in and out of community involvement according to their own circumstances and perceptions, and the demands they face. A socially inclusive information society will have opportunities and access points for people to engage easily with their local or interest community.

It may be that the most significant group of people to keep in mind when considering ICTs and individuals is those who we might describe as 'unclubbable': people who are reluctant or find it difficult to become involved in collective activity or experience. The potential of ICTs to enhance the skills and self-confidence of the unclubbable, and to give them opportunities to engage with others on their own terms and at their own pace, should they wish to, will become one of the key issues for social inclusion in the Information Society.

Community activity and the social economy

Contemporary policy for the regeneration of communities understandably emphasizes employment programmes for economic development. At the same time, of course, community regeneration means local development, and its basis is community activity. As Gabriel Chanan has pointed out, all community activity has developmental value, and all developmental value is economic in the sense of being life-supporting. He explains why there is a need for regeneration programmes to be less narrowly focused on job creation:

> The key connection between community involvement and employment lies in the personal and collective survival strategies of people in disadvantaged localities (or of disadvantaged people in well-off localities). Being or becoming unemployable correlates highly with being localized – by lack of money, fear for safety, care responsibilities etc. This can easily become isolation, which reinforces unemployability. It is through the intimacy, informality and inclusiveness of local community organizations that people can regain the footholds which overcome isolation, give informal education, try out new tasks and responsibilities in an unthreatening environment and gain credibility with local employers.
>
> However, it would be self-defeating to try to cultivate only the explicitly job creating organizations, which are a minority, and ignore the great variety of mutual aid and mutual interest organizations which provide the essential soil for the sector as a whole. It requires a big floor of mutual aid and community involvement to give people the basic conditions to participate in any form of constructive activity, paid or unpaid. Community involvement is also the sustained interface between the local population and public services.[20]

At the same time it is appropriate to stress that ICTs are probably as significant in the social context as in the economic. It may be that the strong popular emphasis on ICTs as a business technology is misplaced.

There are two good reasons why we might claim greater policy recognition for the social contribution of ICTs. First, there is an abundance of evidence, as this book demonstrates, of the technology being used in *transformational* ways in education, arts, health and many of the activities which occupy people in their day-to-day lives. Secondly, as argued above, community activity is fundamental to social and economic regeneration.

A key feature of the information society is the potential for improvements in the efficiencies of the social economy at local level – for example, in the availability of informal and formal support, or in the availability of local information, which can minimize the referred costs of certain social needs. As a recent European study points out:

> There is an evident (though uncosted) economic value to most community activities, not only in equipping people to take economic opportunities but in the substance of the activity itself. It is important to see the continuity between the more obvious economic activities, such as creating a small business, and the less obvious ones, such as providing a free amenity through voluntary labour, reducing individual costs by improving your own housing, or reducing collective costs by negotiating for a new bus service.[21]

Social inclusion in the information society depends on strengthening the social economy. The social economy requires a flourishing community sector – active, well-used community groups which are adequately resourced and which interact appropriately with public authorities. In this context, there are important issues to do with the durability of community groups and their need to keep renewing their membership. Where ICTs are used to bring people together in a neighbourhood – for example in a discussion on the community plan where it is carried out partly online – it will be valuable to explore new ways of sustaining and renewing groups by bringing in new members and new interests and enthusiasm.

A broader policy acceptance of the role of community activity in regeneration would be a great boon for community networking, where the technology enhances the sharing of experience and lessons, where synergies thrive and many of the traditional barriers of disciplines and professions lose their significance.

Strengthening local information and communication networks

In a community which appears not to be healthy, and where the local information ecology is not flourishing and needs reviving, how might it be strengthened?

In the least-integrated and most run-down communities, information exchange may have been reduced to individual and survival issues:

*   accommodation (and communications from landlords)
*   the availability of drugs (and communications with dealers)
*   credit (and communications with lenders) and so on.

In addition, where people are living in fear and trying to escape, there may be several factors which cause particular stagnation in this ecology, such as

*   the lack of opportunities ('occasions') to share news and pass comment;
*   perceived lack of connection between the individual experience and the possibility that collective action could make any difference;
*   lack of an existing flow of *any kind of information* on which new information might be carried (in a silent bus queue or waiting room, people tend not to just start up a conversation out of nothing; yet often, 'nuggets' of useful information are passed on during a conversation which begins with a moan about the weather).

Any ecology depends on an equilibrium between its own autonomy and interaction with the system beyond. As I have argued, a local information network needs nodes where information passes out of, or is imported into, the neighbourhood from the outside world; and communication 'occasions' for the transfer and circulation of information *within* the system. Ecological principles of pollination and receptive conditions apply. In practice, these two functions may be mutually stimulating: pubs and newsagents are good examples. But where people are disinclined or can't afford to go to the pub, or people passing through on their way to work in the morning don't stop at the newsagents, or nobody stands at the bus stop because they've nowhere to go (or there isn't one), then the neighbourhood may be restricted to just two broad forms of information transfer:

- occasional and fairly insular interactions – say, among dog-walkers at the back of a housing estate
- the mass media, which are mostly removed from people's day-to-day lives and provide almost no opportunities for interaction.

In these circumstances the information sub-system may atrophy, with negative consequences for the community as a whole.

There is one town community where an elderly man meets informally with other local people in a baker's shop at half past six in the morning, because that's the only time of day when he feels he can safely cross the road. Such 'gossip' occasions sustain individuals and neighbourhoods mutually, and reinforce the local information ecology. If environmental conditions, or the man's health, deteriorate beyond a certain point, he will no longer be able to participate and the occasion will be correspondingly weakened.

We all recognize that communication requires content, but the importance of occasion is, I suggest, poorly appreciated in community information debates. It may be that one crucial role for ICTs in moribund information environments is to prompt and cause communication by stimulating new options and opportunities.

Stimulating information flow, however, and relating it to the experience of individuals who may have only the most reluctant, and even resentful, association with their neighbourhood, almost certainly calls for skilled intervention. This does not mean that ICTs do not have a hugely significant potential role to play – it seems clear that they have – but that where there are low levels of confidence and collective activity, the key requirement is for a platform of community organization. The issue then is to ensure that community development principles and experience (which is abundant) should be interwoven as thoroughly as possible with the efforts of community networkers.

In this respect, we need to stress more strongly the potential role of community resource centres (CRCs),[22] where people can go to explore the technology, as more critical to social inclusion than home access or Internet use by small businesses, for example. Establishing a network of CRCs could depend on the extent to which it is possible to identify locations which have the potential to become the *default* focus for communication occasions. My contention is that where such a facility is in place, and local people identify their own potential uses of the technology, then other uses of ICTs in helping to sustain community activity – such as providing car-pooling software, or cultural groups generating their own web pages – will follow more naturally.

While we can anticipate certain changes in the uses of technology, it has long been assumed that television will remain the most readily accessed medium, along with the telephone, and that therefore Internet access via digital TV will give a significant boost to access and the use of online communication. If this is so – and there are doubts[23] – there could be a strong case for some kind of regulation which ensures that the local 'community pages' become the default screens on all such systems. The community pages could be provided according to guidelines and monitored standards by a non-profit organization in every locality (defined by certain local government criteria). The pages would provide links to a range of locally determined content and resources, at a point before users entered the world of 'grand central media'.

Project outcomes and social policy

The first age of community networking in the UK has been shaped significantly by the project culture. Some of the implications of this, in areas such as funding, partnership and sustainability, have been considered in the COMMIT report published in 1997.[24] We can now see more clearly how such a culture requires a broader understanding of project outcomes. We need to seek clearer recognition in policy of causal relationships between local development activity (community development, community activity, providing independent learning environments, providing supported access to communication channels etc) and genuine social change.

The policy challenge for community networkers and community librarians is to explain the relationship between *outputs* (which may be identifiable, measurable and within the domain of project workers) and *outcomes* which legitimately may be unanticipated, the result of a complex combination of coincidental factors, and beyond the subject scope of those involved.

For example, community development work which stimulates voluntary activity to establish a computer resource for young people, and provides them with somewhere to go, may contribute indirectly to reduced fear of crime in a neighbourhood, without this being an expressed aim of the work. By extension, the project may also contribute to enhanced social cohesion. But a worker on a young people's ICT access project cannot necessarily be expected to have expertise in crime policy, and reduced fear of crime may be the result of various quite independent actions.

While several pioneers have begun invaluable work here,[25] we still lack the tools to demonstrate the connections between broader social objectives and the kinds of exploratory, developmental processes which have uncertain, diffused outcomes. There is increasing evidence of policy receptivity to such arguments. But projects need to be less burdened by the old shackles of quantitative outputs, and given confidence to explore and demonstrate their contribution to broader outcomes. Such confidence and understanding is likely to be found in the best area-based partnerships sooner than anywhere else.

Concluding remarks

What is at issue, then, is the reconfiguration of communities in the information society. The information society is considerably more than the technology and its uses. It's about new kinds of social relationships, cross-sectoral partnerships, changes in the social location of information, and potentially significant changes in patterns of communication. (It is no accident that debate about the information society has increased at a time when the structural nature of disadvantage and social inclusion is increasingly acknowledged in policy programmes: both developments are characteristic of an age where artificial barriers which constrain the way people work and behave, and respond to problems, are being broken down.) To what extent will these and other features of the information society allow for the development of new community strengths, and the reinforcement of existing strengths? To what extent will they enable communities to adjust, and to control their adjustment in a sustainable way?

John Hobcraft, writing on behalf of the Centre for the Analysis of Social Exclusion,[26] has drawn attention to the significance of five childhood predictors of exclusion in adult life:

- childhood poverty
- family disruption
- contact with the police before age 16
- educational test scores, and
- father's interest in schooling.

It is important to echo his reminder in the same report that these are aggregate tendencies and in no sense determinist: 'There is huge scope for many, if not most, individuals to escape from the patterns and tendencies observed.'[27] We need to be exploring and explaining how ICTs can contribute to such escapes. But individual solutions may not be community solutions, and we need to go much further, by presenting the argument that ICTs can transform the context of exclusion by helping neighbourhoods to become more integrated, by being used to stimulate and sustain community activity. There are plenty of early innovative examples which are showing the way in addressing family involvement or promoting educational attainment. On the Pennywell estate in Sunderland, for example, young people are told that their 'ticket' to attend an ICT training course is to bring a parent or grandparent with them;[28] young people excluded from school in Knowsley are offered an alternative computer-based curriculum of their own choice based in a public library, helping them to acquire skills for social integration with adults other than teachers, where neither the technology nor the library are associated with previous failure;[29] at Blakeston in Stockton, school pupils in danger of becoming excluded attended a 'Skills for Life' course which includes basic IT, and excelled in subsequent school examinations.[30]

We must be wary of quickfix technological solutions, particularly where conflict between communities and authorities exists. The 'community' is not necessarily right in its view, nor are officers or professionals necessarily right in theirs. We have to resist the 'rosetinting' of 'the community': many communities are riddled with conflict, and to present them as harmonious could be a dangerous dismissal of need. What's needed is not instant email access to decision-makers for articulate and well-connected residents, but a mutual space for residents, and for those with responsibility for what happens in a locality, to filter and absorb information, and to convert it into appropriate knowledge and action. E-mail, after all, is only one device among various available to us. As we learn to use discussion lists and links to supporting material more effectively, it is reasonable that we should aspire to decision-making processes which reflect a better-informed, more empowering and more responsible democratic process.

The ethos of community information implies the deinstitutionalization of knowledge.[31] The same could be said of this technology. To exploit ICTs fully, we need the fullest possible understanding of how communication takes place at local level, together with a strong policy commitment to community activity.

References

1   *The net result: social inclusion in the information society: report of the National Working Party on Social Inclusion* (INSINC), IBM UK and CDF, 1997, para 3.28–3.34. Available at
    <http://www.uk.ibm.com/comm/community/uk117.html>
2   Tannen, D, *The argument culture: changing the way we argue and debate*, Virago, 1998, 247.
3   *Bringing Britain together: a national strategy for neighbourhood renewal: report by the Social Exclusion Unit*, Cm4045, London, The Stationery Office, 1998.
4   <http://www.pat15.org.uk>
5   'Foreword by the Prime Minister', *Bringing Britain together*, op cit, 7.
6   Barr, A, Hashagen, S and Purcell, R, *Monitoring and evaluation of community development in Northern Ireland*, Scottish Community Development Centre, 1996.
    Barr, A, Hashagen, S and Purcell, R, *Measuring community development in*

Northern Ireland: a handbook for practitioners, Scottish Community Development Centre, 1996. Available at <http://www.scdc.org.uk/nessup/hand3.html>

7   *Measuring community development in Northern Ireland*, 10–11.

8   This and subsequent sections draw heavily on: Harris, K, Information and communication in the community sector, *Information management in the voluntary sector*, London, Aslib, 1998, 59–72.

9   Op cit, para 3.12.

10   Harris, K, Freedom of access to information. In *Informing communities*, Kinnell, M (ed), Newcastle, Staffs, CSG Publishing, 1992, 55–7.

11   Castel, R, *De l'indigence a l'exclusion*, 1991, cited in *Community involvement in urban regeneration: added value and changing values*, Luxembourg, Office for Official Publications of the European Communities, 1997, 38.

12   Carrying out research in Auchinleck in 1997, I was told that there are families who have lived there for generations, and seldom go anywhere else: 'they'll no' venture into other areas . . . People are comfortable and happy to be in their village . . . it's comfort zones.' (Harris, K, *Open to interpretation: community perceptions of the social benefits of public libraries*, CDF, 1998, 30). Evidence for this 'habit of isolation' has been confirmed in various subsequent project visits around the country. For example, I was told of experience at a school in Speke, Merseyside, where most children apparently had never been to Liverpool City Centre.

13   Shearman, C, *Local connections: making the net work for neighbourhood renewal*, Communities Online, 1999, para 2.10.

14   Seenan, G, Snatched from jaws of Pilton's poverty trap, *The Guardian*, 3 December 1998, 11.

15   Shaddock, J, Barnsley MBC, personal communication, August 1998.

16   Grunwald, T, *Making the net work: on-line strategies for community-based organisations*, North Carolina, NCexChange, 1997. Published in the UK by Partnerships Online. Available at <http://www.partnerships.org.uk>

17   Op cit, para 6.11.

18   Wellman, B and Gulia, M, *Net surfers don't ride alone: virtual communities as communities*, University of Toronto, April 1996. Available at <http://www.chass.utoronto.ca:8080/~wellman/index.html>

19   Cited in *The net result*, op cit, para 2.31.

20 Chanan, G, *Community involvement: promoting best practice*, Dublin, European Foundation for the Improvement of Living and Working Conditions, 1999.

21 *Community involvement in urban regeneration*, op cit, 39.

22 *The net result*, op cit, para 5.18–5.27.

23 Cawson, A, Lewis, J, *Report summarising academic research and public domain market research on attitudes to and use of information technologies in the home*, Department of Trade and Industry, 1999.

24 Day, P and Harris, K, *Down-to-earth vision: community based IT initiatives and social inclusion*. IBM and CDF, 1997. Available at **<http://www.uk.ibm.com/comm/community/uk171.html>**

25 See for example, Francois Matarasso, *Use or ornament? The social impact of participation in the arts*, Comedia, 1997; Linley, R and Usherwood, R, *New measures for the new library: a social audit of public libraries*, Department of Information Studies, University of Sheffield, 1998.

26 Hobcraft, J, *Intergenerational and life-course transmission of social exclusion: influences of childhood poverty, family disruption, and contact with the police*, London, Centre for the Analysis of Social Exclusion, November 1998. Available at **<http://sticerd.lse.ac.uk/Case/default.htm>**

27 Ibid.

28 Tulip, J, Pennywell Community Business, personal communication, 4 February 1999.

29 The Outlook Project, Knowsley Library Service, 5th Floor, Municipal Buildings, Archway road, PO Box 22, Huyton, Knowsley L36 9YX. Knowsley, Lancashire, 1998.

30 Bell, M, Community Tutor, Blakeston School, personal communication, 9 February 1999.

31 Martin, W J, *Community librarianship: changing the face of public libraries*, London, Library Association Publishing, 1989.

7

Inside out
The shape of New Library

JOHN DOLAN

Early in 1997 the Government invited the Library and Information Commission to report, by the summer of that year, on a plan to network public libraries in the UK. It had been recognized during an extended period of reviewing the role and nature of the UK's library service that the accelerating developments in information technology offered new opportunities for the service to formulate a development path which would take it into the next century – or millennium, depending on your choice of rhetoric. The result was the report submitted to Government at the end of July and published in October. The Secretary of State for Culture, Chris Smith, in the New Labour Government, in power since the May of that year, said that the report represented 'a defining moment' for library services in the UK. *New Library: The people's network*[1] had captured the imagination and enthusiasm of all who read it.

New Library: The people's network was almost entirely forward looking. It dwelt little on the long history of public libraries. Only in its end papers, with a smattering of salient facts and figures, did it attempt to 'justify' the library service – its scale, variety and usage. Instead, it grasped a vision of society in the information age and presented with a flourish the concept of a library service which would be re-positioned and re-equipped for the era ahead.

'New Library' network

Part of the purpose, nonetheless, of building a 'New Library' network would be to build on the library's past. Using the widely dispersed network of over 4000 outlets, their popularity, their independence as centres for information and learning, the network would be a 'people's network': a place to access 'virtually' everything that new technology could deliver; a centre for community communications; an inclusive entry point which would level the playing field between those who had access to networks and those without. Moreover, it would be an entry point not merely to the network but to dedicated networked information resources, to government and to the interactive exchange of knowledge and opinion, information and services.

New Library: The people's network recognized the supreme value of the content – information, knowledge, services – to be delivered, and in analysing this in several strands highlighted, as a key strategic need, 'Citizens' information and involvement in society':

> A healthy society must also communicate with itself, and the UK Public Library Network will not only provide access to the centres of administration but will enable people to interact with all manner of voluntary organizations and interest groups. In addition, local government will be able to use the network to consult residents affected by local issues of policy, planning and prioritisation. When citizens are openly and freely in communication with government, democracy can be said to have 'grown up'.[1]

Idealism

Where the previous UK Government had been criticized for too close an adherence to ideology, the new one came in on a wave of idealism. This idealism for a modern, inclusive and participative democracy was captured in the report in a vision for a new kind of library which would help to facilitate radical change. This was reflected in the Government's formal response[2] and in the Prime Minister's introduction to *Our Information Age: The Government's vision*[3] in April 1998. Significant Government policy priorities have informed both the plan for a networked library service and the positive reaction from Government:

1   **Economic prosperity**: Only through the widest access for a reskilled nation can the UK prosper in a global economy where suc-

cess is based on information, communications, service and cultural industries.

2   **Education**: The key to economic prosperity and a better quality of life.

3   **Modern government**: Devolution combined with accessibility and a people enabled to take part.

4   **Lifelong learning**: All the above policies informed by a culture in which learning is desirable and not a drudge.

Targets

Our Information Age set targets (mostly the year 2002) for networking public services, notably schools, in a 'national grid for learning' that included libraries. Alongside the University for Industry, with others, the 'New Library' will deliver learning opportunities and support business success as well as personal and community development.

By the end of 1998, funding has been identified from the New Opportunities Fund of the National Lottery to create content for the New Library network and to implement the original report's plan for the training of all library staff – some 35,000 people mostly, in daily face-to-face encounters with the people.

This latter issue reflects the challenge of realism in the face of idealism which fired *New Library: The people's network*. While the report expresses the opportunities of the future it addresses the means of getting there. In no sense will this be an easy transition. Moreover, it is not solely dependent on the library changing. Our society, how it operates and communciates with itself, will have to change too if the envisaged accessibility of the people's network is to be exploited by people who are keen to learn, enthusiastic about participation and positive about a sense of inclusion.

Major change is a challenge to any organization. National change on this scale presents phenomenal tasks for cultural, managerial and operational transformation – for example:

1   The public library is popular but there is still evidence that, although it is widely used, there are important sectors of the community where there is only a minor sense of affinity.

2   The public library usually delivers 'content' created by others. Content creation will be, for most librarians, a new responsibility.
3   The infusion of locally based access to a national/international network into all libraries will have a transforming impact, exploding the smallest library into a local global access point and opening the biggest to a worldwide community of speculation and inquiry.
4   The role of the library as a place where the excluded gain access will bring people to libraries but with a new expectation of the 'supportive environment' offering information and guidance, help with learning, assistance in access and support through the evaluation of limitless sources. This will give library staff an active responsibility rather than a passive duty. It will be more exciting but it will be different.

However, such a library will help realize the economic, educational and social ideals which lie behind the Government's aspirations. These too, on a grander scale, will require a sea change in society.

Changing scene

The UK is richer than it was 30 years ago but it is also – and this is more significant – more diverse.

The wider span between rich and poor, cultural diversity in a religious and ethical maze, changes in technology and industry, employment and training, new and different family values and structures – these and other factors will mitigate against cohesion, consistency and continuity. It is already harder to anticipate the needs of each and every library user. The expectations of an increasingly multifaceted community can only be anticipated generically, even philosophically, while political aspiration will always, ultimately, determine priorities by virtue of their impact on the voter.

The environment into which the New Library will be delivered will be more challenging in itself than any organizational change within the library and information community. Take three areas, for example:

1   **Modern government**: This is an aspiration to combat a growing lack of nterest in government, politics and community affairs,

while 'managing the nation' itself is transformed by devolution for the Home Countries, new structures for regional administration and development in England, a new kind of government for London and the push–pull tension of the UK's position within the EU.

2   **Social inclusion**: In the face of alienation and poverty, many initiatives, especially since the 1970's, have failed to create a unified society of equal opportunity. Project upon project has meant only local or partial change. Inclusion must mean inclusion for all members of society within their own community. This would surely require such synergy of purpose – for Government departments, voluntary organizations, public services and the private sector – that even 'joined up thinking', to use the current phraseology, will need to be superseded by a fusion of planning and action of still uncertain proportions.

3   **Economic prosperity**: Even in the global society this still represents success in competition. Nation competes with nation or, perhaps, federation with continent with 'united states'. Success will still derive from investment, and will therefore continue to be built on a spiral of economic growth. The investment needed will be increasingly intense infrastructure, skills, innovation, production, marketing.

Our global society is one characterized not only by harmony and more heterogeneous, pervasive communications, but also by more diversity of interest, purpose and goal.

Future positive?

How will the library of the future serve the emerging society? The Government's response to *New Library: The people's network* included the allocation of funding – £50 million for the creation of original digital content and £20 million for the training of library staff. With these – for libraries – unprecedented funding awards came another request to the Library and Information Commission for a further report giving guidance to the New Opportunities Fund on how these resources should be distributed.

Published in November 1998, *Building the New Library network*[4] fulfilled this request. A report, as substantial as the first, set out the priorities accompanied by an array of 18 appendices, with, among others, background on international trends, the principles of lifelong learning, and an analysis of staff training needs. The guidance on content development identified three main strands: cultural enrichment, citizens' information and involvement, and re-skilling the nation. The report recommended accredited quality training for all employees to achieve the 'European Computer Driving Licence', combined with advanced training for staff with selected developmental roles and responsibilities.

While the new digital content promises an array of learning resources delivered free at the point of use to every library, the training programme, over three years, promises the most dramatic impact ever known on the UK-wide library workforce.

Library inside out

While the task of undertaking this development programme promises, in the best sense, to turn the public library community upside down, the effect will be to turn the library inside out.

1   **The library's contribution to modernizing government**: Modern government will depend on a refreshed democracy, a new broad-based and informed interest in the processes of governance based on awareness, information, access to and between people and institutions, and the responsive interactive delivery of services. The library will be a place for

    • access to the New Library network and the wider Internet
    • learning resources about how government works and how to intervene
    • communications direct to centres of power and between geographical and interest communities.

    Staff will be enablers, interpreters and educators. Library organizations will partner with voluntary and community-based organizations in content creation, and will actively promote knowledge, understanding and involvement.

2   **The library's contribution to social inclusion**: Inclusion is not conformity. It should be about flexible adapted policies and services, and will require a change in the bureaucracy and in the delivery of services and institutions. They will need to recognize, at last, and respond to, the unstoppable dismembering of traditions, stereotypes and norms which is reforming society into a pluralistic, classless dynamo of activity and relationships. More than 4000 libraries may be community-based access points. But they must also re-form into agents for the external delivery and promotion of information and learning opportunities. Creating and delivering content to libraries is one aim. Ultimately, the library without walls will be accessed from the home, school, community or health centre. From the library network will spin out a community-oriented web of new resources responsive to diverse social, educational and cultural needs, interests and expectations.

3   **The library's contribution to economic prosperity**: Living in the information age, people will only experience prosperity if they have the skills and confidence to access and exploit the complex web of information and learning opportunities. A newly skilled library workforce will facilitate access to learning resources designed to disseminate ability to people of all ages and backgrounds. Libraries will be vehicles not only for delivering learning but also for promoting the desire to learn which is the aspiration of Government and others in the UK's drive towards a prosperous future.

The lottery investment in digital content, staff training and the dissemination of skills will need to be accompanied by parallel changes in the character and operation of libraries.

Equal partnership

From policy level to service delivery, the library organization will have to be re-established as an equal partner alongside the education system, industry, the media and communications services, voluntary and pressure groups. It will have to be unprecedentedly focused and re-marketed to concentrate on clearly stated objectives for serving a wider, bigger audience, through new delivery mechanisms operating from within and in partnership with the community.

The new resources will not be sufficient on their own. Funding for the infrastructure (at January 1999) remains to be identified. Further budgets will be needed for more training, marketing, the re-equipping of buildings, and the constant maintenance and replacement of IT equipment.

Above all, the decline in opening hours which has accelerated in recent years must be reversed if accessibility is to be a meaningful objective. Across the UK, the disparate management of libraries by over 200 local authorities will need coordination and collaboration at regional, national and UK levels. The library will be open all hours – by virtual access through day and night – and must be open all days of the week for maximum effectiveness.

The vision of the 'New Library' has won over library leaders; staff are, with increased awareness, taking up the challenge enthusiastically.

Outside the library community, partner organizations, current users and the still-large body of non-users must be persuaded to detach themselves from the drab library stereotype and share the ambition for a new kind of library which creates and promotes knowledge as well as acquires it, and which demolishes the walls that house collections to build new structures for the active dispersal of the wonders of the human mind.

References

1   *New Library: The people's network*, Library and Information Commission, London 1997. Available at
    <http://www.ukoln.ac.uk/services/lic/newlibrary/>
2   *New Library: The people's network: The Government's Response* (Cm 3887), The Stationery Office.
3   *Our Information Age: The Government's Vision*, 1998. Available at
    <http://www.number-10.gov.uk>
4   *Building the New Library network*, London, Library and Information Commission, 1998.

8

European city model
Barcelona Community Network (BCNet)

Artur Serra

The BCNet experience: Starting a local and European CIN simultaneously

In April 1996, Barcelona Community Networking (BCNet) started as an initiative from several local institutions in the city, among them the Universitat Politecnica de Catalunya (UPC). The idea at the beginning was to offer some computer facilities to civic institutions beyond the campus. At the same time, we at the university wanted to explore community networking as a new research field.[1]

This initiative was a part of EPITELIO,[2] one of the first European projects focused on telecommunications applications against social exclusion. BCNet's approach from the beginning was that the best way to start a civic network was to promote social inclusion. That initiative was accepted, and EPITELIO actually became the first European project to promote community networking in different countries, in particular Spain, Italy and the UK Fiorella di Cindio from the Università di Milano and Bernard Leach from Manchester Metropolitan University also participated according to the same philosophy.

Another distinctive aspect of BCNet was that from very beginning of the project we entered an open dialogue with the city authorities of Barcelona in order to secure their support. As is well known, Barcelona is one of the founding cities of the European consortium called 'Telecities'.[3] This consortium was proposed by Manchester and established in 1993 as a means of drawing the attention of the EU to the opportunities provided by telecommunications applications in the cities. From the beginning, we thought that community networking needed to be open to the participation of the city authorities, who, surprisingly, took an attentive but passive attitude towards our efforts. The process of convincing them that we were working as a public service, promoted on a voluntary basis and for the benefit of the city, took more time that we had anticipated. But this was not the only surprise of the project.

How to create a CIN in a metropolitan city

From the beginning we were concerned about the insurmountable problems presented by the creation of a CIN in a metropolitan city of 3 million people (with 1.5 million in the central area). We visited National Capital Freenet in Canada in the summer of 1996, and we talked with Dave Sutherland, Kyla Huckerby and other leading representatives of this huge CIN, but although we thought we never could raise the money and the computer resources they had, we still wanted to build a CIN in Barcelona.

Fortunately, 1996 saw the explosion of the Internet, and the prices for basic services became really competitive. For £5 sterling a month some non-profit services like Pangea[4] provided basic Internet services to non governmental organizations (NGOs) and other non-profit associations. The usual problem of providing basic Internet connectivity was not a major concern for our CIN. We started to provide free access to local organizations in order to focus on the creation of community networking and to optimize our limited resources. Our research team then gained the assistance of a shared server located at the Telecommunications Engineering School and a voluntary graduate student to help to continue the work.

Given that Barcelona is so big, how were we to begin the task of creating BCNet? We started to work by districts and by neighbourhoods. Central Barcelona was divided in the 1980s into ten districts of approximately 150,000 citizens each. A clear local policy towards decentralization was implemented. We had some contacts with the richly diverse web in Nou Barris, a working-class district in the north east of the city. Another enthusiastic group of young activists, organized into a cultural association called TRIA Nou Barris, grasped the idea quickly and started up as Nou Barris Net, so two district CINs were now linked to BCNet.[5]

These people are in charge of the local district TV channel, so they immediately started a TV programme, *BCN Digital*, on community networking and other digital news. They raised some funding and bought some computers for starting courses on the Internet and CINs. They gained expertise in that field and developed some courses for the municipal department in charge of civic organizations, which is located in Torre Jussana. More than 100 people from several local associations have attended these courses.

Spontaneous growth

However, the process, though promising, was really slow. We combined activism at the grassroots level with academic activity. We organized a course on CIN in 1996/97 at the university (UPC), which was pretty successful. More than 20 students of computer science and telecommunications engineering attended and learned about CINs. As a result of this, two secondary teachers from TEB, an association for young people in El Raval, came to the UPC and asked for support to start a CIN in their neighbourhood. Whereas most visitors to Barcelona go to Les Ramblas, a lively neighbourhood in the downtown area, El Raval is the poor, marginalized section of downtown Barcelona, despite being right next to Les Ramblas.

In this place, the work of TEB has been incredible. They have developed a community network serving 20 local associations, with some for North African communities originating from Morocco, Algeria and Tunisia. In their community centre they are training a new generation of adolescents, who are discovering for the first time that they can have a place in the new digital age. In 1997 RavalNet won a prize from the regional government as the best initiative for training young people.[6]

We suddenly realized that other initiatives in other districts of Barcelona had grown up spontaneously with their own computer infrastructure, domains and funds. Gracia Net,[7] Sant Andreu Net and Sants Montjuic are already established. This last one has been an initiative of a young retail company of young entrepreneurs who sell hardware and software. These people started a website called Sants Montjuic only as a local information point in the Net. We contacted them and offered the possibility of evolving towards a district CIN. They agreed and received the support of the district authorities. Now they are establishing a sustainable CIN, called Xarxa 3 (Net 3) after the number of their district, with their own domain[8] and the support of a coordinated body of more than 100 associations from this district.

A local, regional, national and global movement

Two years on, we are in the process of establishing BCNet as a decentralized community network, serving several hundreds organizations in the city of Barcelona. Our attention is now focused on organizing an independent non-profit agency made up of public and private donors in order to create sustainable growth and a degree of permanence.

We see CINs as being diverse and pluralistic as our society as a whole. This is why we have promoted the Catalan coordination of the different CINs which are currently working. A first meeting of Spanish CINs was held in September in Cuenca,[9] and we have also organized a number of European conferences of CINs.

As part of a European project, we have worked for two years with a very clear orientation towards international cooperation. A community network is based on local communication, of course, but the global nature of the media they use, Internet, allows them to open up to the world. For the first time, local communities can be global in the sense that we promote the coordination of CINs firstly in Europe and then globally. In 1997, Rete Civiche di Milano and BCNet organized the First European Conference on Community Networking. It took place in Milan, Italy, and was the first European conference to gather participants from the most developed networks such as Freenet Finland, Digital Staats from Amsterdam and Communities on Line from the UK.[10]

The second European Conference on CIN was in Barcelona. This time people were invited from all over the world. Telecommunities Canada, Association for Community Networking from USA,[11] VicNet from Australia, Friends and Partners from Russia, and of course the people from the European Association for CINS.[12]

Next Generation Community Networking: CINs as digital cities, digital cities as CINs

For the first time, the city authorities of Barcelona have openly and generously supported this kind of event. They are beginning to talk about 'civic participation'. They even have started an area in the city web for sending mails to the Mayor.

As the CIN has grown, two phenomena have simultaneously appeared:

1   The idea of a digital city has started to be looked at again in the light of civic participation and digital democracy. Politicians have begun to understand that community networking can be a political issue just like traffic jams or smoke contamination.
2   The community networks have begun to take on more and more political responsibilities. They need to think big, not only in hundreds of associations but in hundreds of thousands of citizens. The idea of a Universal Net Service has arisen, as well as the possibility of a local net connecting the whole city like the electricity or water system.

In short, as CINs tends to become digital cities, so digital cities will tend to become CINs. This convergence is what we call **Next Generation Community Networking**.

The design of a new generation of community networks is on the table. It is possible that a CIN could include 90% of the population of a city? What are the computer, economic, social and cultural issues to be addressed when designing such large systems? Are we ready, as the CIN research community, to think about these issues? Is there a real CIN research community yet?

Fiorella di Cindio, L Navarro and A Serra promoted the first workshop on community networking as a new research field, which took place during the ECSCW'97 Conference in Lancaster.[13] A second one was planned by the same three people plus Doug Schuler at the 1998 PDC Conference in Seattle, US.

Some of the research problems we are working on are

- the relationship of CINs to the Next Generation Internet, community networking and universal services
- architectures for large-scale cooperation at the local level.

Next Generation Internet: a technology for community networking

The current Internet was not planned to connect everybody, but Next Generation Internet (NGI) will do this, although at present there is a division between the NGI research community and the CIN movement. We do not have any experience yet of plans to link CINs through GigaPops.

Some EU bodies such as the Internet Society European Coordinating Council are discussing the possibility of establishing high-speed networks at the local, national and European level connected to CINs.[14]

Internet 2 will allow a broadband Internet at home, as well as at the civic authority and community network levels. It is generally understood that the level of computer literacy is in inverse proportion to the speed of the network. The more literate the user is, the less speed is required. Simple e-mail and conferencing systems were enough in the pioneering times of the Net. Companies are satisfied with a low-level website, together with some graphics and sound facilities for publishing and advertising. But the general public, the ordinary citizen, needs broadband services like video-conferencing, full multimedia Net, and a simple keyboard or none at all. These applications need QoS, new traffic management tools etc for the Next Generation Internet technologies.

But who is interested in an information society (we stress the word 'society')? Obviously the EU member states. The real beneficiary of the NGI will be the country, or alliance of countries, interested in providing access to the Net for every citizen. This is the way to achieve a universal net service.

The Internet Civic Address Service: a first step

The idea of a universal net service is a big plus factor in community net-working. In fact, CIN promoters can present themselves as the main champions of such an idea. But how can we offer realistic steps in that direction? The public authorities are no longer the owners of the tele-com infrastructure: how can we combine public benefits with the pri-vate commercial interests?

We are now thinking in CANet, the Centre for Internet Applications at the University here in Barcelona,[15] of establishing an Internet Civic Address Service (ICAS), which will contain the local Internet address of every citizen in our community – eg 'first name'.'family name'@district.city.nation – which will complement the Internet Professional Address (IPA) given by a company, university or ISP. The ICA is the Internet address which should be given by local authorities to every citizen, in every democratic city, in order to fulfil the basic requirements for digital citizenship, and it provides the con-ditions for an extensive electronic market. It is founded on a local dem-ocratic culture that organizes the cities according to residential addresses. Now Internet is the new digital space for creating digital communities. We want to join the democratic culture with the high-tech culture.

Within Internet, this local service can be expanded to include every democratic country worldwide – an Internet version of the universal services provided by the postal and telephone networks.

What are the goals of ICAS?

It provides

- a service to promote the e-market in your community
- a way to enhance local communities in the information age
- a good opportunity for ISPs to enlarge their market.

But also runs the danger of

- allowing local authorities to control their citizens like 'Big Brother'
- creating an explosion in the spamming (unwanted mail) industry.

How does an ICAS work?

Technically, the whole system can be considered as a big alias system. You can carry out the following step by step:

1   You can create an Internet directory of citizens (based on the local census), including citizen data such as names, address and also the IPA. The implementation can be based on X.500 or LDAP, supported mainly by the local authorities.
2   You can reserve a city domain as a neutral domain for every member of your community (it is not the property of the city authorities). This domain will define the Internet Civic Addresses.
3   You can create a redirection service that forwards messages from ICA to IPA. This service can be supported by a new organization or by the same ISPs.
4   You can protect the identity of users with a digital certificate (issued by a public certification board) that will provide the proper security and confidentiality for members, plus additional measures to avoid any misuse of the service (junk mail, spamming etc.).

Politically, the development of an ICA service requires

*   a communal public debate about it
*   a public–private partnership based on a civic organization with the participation of the local authority plus local interested parties (companies, ISP, universities) to develop the system
*   an organization to manage the service, funded by all interested parties.

Economically, the service needs to offer business opportunities to the local telecom operators:

1   Local authorities need not provide the Internet connectivity but can provide the citizen directory and partially support the redirection service.
2   Internet service providers will provide the Internet connections, and partially support of redirection service.
3   A public certification board needs to be defined.

Finally, with regard to new architectures for large-scale cooperation, we are working towards the establishment of LocalNets[16] as an open architecture connecting all the local IP networks in a cooperative platform of applications and services.

The way is now open to the design of a new generation of community networks.

References

1 <http://www.canet.upc.es/ws>
2 <http://www.epitelio.org>
3 <http://www.edc.eu.int>
4 <http://www.pangea.org>
5 < http://www.bcnet.upc.es/9bnet>
6 <http://www.bcnet.upc.es/ravalnet>
7 <http://www.gracianet.org/welcome.shtml>
8 <http://www.xarxa3.org>
9 <http://www.epitelio.org>
10 <http://www.bcnet.upc.es/ecn97>
11 <http://bcn.boulder.co.us/afcn/>
12 <http://www.bcnet.upc.es/ecn98>
13 <http://www.bcnet.upc.es/ws>
14 <http://www.canet. upc.es/isoc-eu-ngi. html>
15 <http://www.canet.upc.es>
16 <http://www.canet.upc.es/localnet.html>

9

City model
Cambridge Online City

MIKE HOSKING

Project background

Cambridge Online City is an initiative started by Anne Campbell MP in 1995, aiming to increase access to public information through the use of technology. This arose from a fear that, as the information society and use of the Internet took off, those without the appropriate skills or access to the right equipment would be left behind.

One of the strengths of the project from the outset was the partnership of different groups and organizations committed to that objective, and the project has had the support of local businesses, public authorities, the voluntary sector and individuals.

Since the initial launch the project has pursued a number of complementary goals:

- the installation of free public access terminals at sites around Cambridge
- the creation of pages of useful, locally relevant information
- training and awareness raising
- support, encouragement and publication of information by community groups.

The project now employs two part-time development workers and has the support a host of volunteer trainers, web authors and other volunteers.

In certain areas the project has focused on different sections of the community in more depth, and has just launched a dedicated training centre for people with disabilities. Specialized equipment and software is available and a trainer is on hand to help people learn how to use it.

Another initiative worked with Cambridge YouthNet to visit youth groups and help them develop and publish material on the Web.

The project has recently been successful in obtaining sponsorship from various sources, including a sizeable grant from the National Lotteries Charity Board. The project is a registered company, and has applied for charitable status.

Public access

Free public access to the Internet has been a key part of the project from the outset, providing access to facilities for those who do not have computers at home or at work. From the first site in 1995, the network of terminals has grown to 18 across Cambridge, with funding in place to increase this to 24 over the coming year. The initial installations have recently been upgraded to the latest Pentium PCs with 17 inch screens, CD-ROMs, speakers and printers.

Training courses at the terminals have proved extremely popular and are booked well in advance.

The terminals are located city-wide at the following places:

- City Housing Office, 89 Cherry Hinton Road
- Citizens Advice Bureau, 72/74 Newmarket Road
- Citizens Advice Bureau, Concourse, Addenbrookes Hospital
- Arbury Court Library
- Lion Yard Library
- Cambridge Council for Voluntary Service, Regent Street (for use by voluntary groups)
- Buchan Street Community Centre
- The Meadows Community Centre
- Newton Cucumber Youth Centre
- Centre 33 – a young people's advice centre
- The Guildhall, Cambridge City Council
- Worker Opportunities through Self Help
- Cherry Hinton Library

- Milton Road Library
- Newmarket Road Library
- Rock Road Library.

The website

This has changed in nature since the start of the project. At the outset there was little locally relevant information available on the Internet and the bulk of what was to be found was provided by the University, and aimed at its students. There was a clear need at that stage to pro-vide easy-to-find information on accommodation, benefits and employment, as well as entertainment and tourism.

As use of the Internet has developed, the project has seen its role less as being the prime source for that information, and more as a gateway to information maintained elsewhere. As an example, we have moved from maintaining a comprehensive directory of 'what's on' informa-tion to providing pointers to some of the numerous other sites aiming to cover that information.

The interest of the project in this area in now much more in in the information available through other routes.

The second major strand to our use of the Web has been as a forum for community involvement and publishing. Dozens of community groups have been able to publish information on the Internet through the resources of the project. This has been achieved in a variety of ways, including using volunteers to create Web pages for certain groups, through to simply hosting sites and providing technical advice for those willing to try Web page writing themselves.

Recent additions have included pages for

- Centre 33 – the young people's advisory service
- the University of the Third Age
- a major directory of resources and opportunities for a youth volun-teering project
- a neighbourhood trust
- an eating disorders organization
- a local AIDS awareness campaign
- Cambridge Racial Incidents Support Project

- Cambridge African Association
- Cambridge Refugee Support Group
- Speaking Up Advocacy Service
- Cambridgeshire Alcohol Advisory Service
- a Sitting Service for Children with Special Needs.

The other information provided includes

- community information (a searchable index of over 4000 voluntary and self-help groups, clubs and societies)
- an A–Z guide to council services
- accommodation in Cambridge (including lists of accommodation agencies and Wintercomfort Scheme)
- benefits offices addresses and helplines
- 'what's on' in the Cambridge area
- job vacancies – links to some vacancy databases and the WOTS (Worker Opportunities Through Self-help) organization
- general information on Cambridge City
- links to other Intemet resources.

The website can be found at **<http://www.worldserver.pipex.com/ cambridge/>**

With sponsorship from a local web design company, a major redesign and expansion of the site is planned for 1999.

Projects

Pathways project

Cambridge Online City has recently launched the Pathways project to support disabled users wishing to learn IT skills, with funding from Cambridge City Council.

In 1998 a major exhibition of adaptive technology was organized in Cambridge, with suppliers demonstrating how their hardware and software solutions could help disabled users make use of IT.

In February 1999, the project launched a dedicated training centre for disabled users in Cambridge, with voice recognition and other software, specialized keyboards and mice. Interest so far has been keen. Free sessions can be booked with the professional trainer at the centre, who will show users how they can make the most of IT, and train them to use common packages.

Youthnet

The Cambridge YouthNet project is another initiative supported by Cambridge Online City.

This has involved young people in producing their own material for the Internet, involving them in writing, designing and publishing material on the Web, with the assistance of a youth worker employed for the purpose. An initial set of pages was produced in 1998.

The project is now entering a new phase, with a partnership with Ad-hoc Publishing to develop this work further, providing youth groups around the City with the training and technical facilities to create and update more material on the Web.

Training

Training has been central to the project from the start. Initially the emphasis was on 'training the trainers', ensuring that staff and materials were on hand to guide novice users through their first steps on the Internet.

Since the appointment of the project development workers we have had the opportunity to harness teams of volunteers keen to participate in the project, by training them to be volunteer trainers. There are now sessions arranged at most of the Cambridge Online City venues, and they are heavily subscribed.

The new machines now being installed also have CD-ROMs installed, able to run training materials for those unused to using computers, or who cannot manage to get to a training session.

Paper-based guidance and training material is also on hand at all of the outlets.

Partners

The project has been supported in time and effort by a large range of voluntary, public and commercial bodies. Both Cambridgeshire County Council and Cambridge City Council have been heavily involved in providing project management, data and technical skills.

One of the unique strengths of the project has been the partnership of these bodies and individuals working together to further the aims of the project.

Sponsors include

- Unipalm-Pipex
- Cambridge Cable
- Cap Gemini
- Software AG
- BBC Education
- Halifax bank
- Kan Design
- Leopart PR
- Mediation Technology
- Multimedia Generation Ltd
- Toby Churchill
- Cambridge Council for Voluntary Service
- University of Cambridge Local Examinations Syndicate
- University of Cambridge
- Anglia Polytechnic University
- Acorn Online Media
- Cambridge and Huntingdon Health Authority
- Cambridgeshire County Council
- Cambridge City Council
- National Lottery Charities Board
- Quest Science Centre.

Patrons

The Project's patrons are Anne Campbell MP, Lord Hoilick, Prof Stephen Hawking and Sir Charles Chadwyck-Healey.

URL, e-mail and address

The Cambridge Online website uniform resouce locator (URL) is **<http://www.worldserver.pipex.com/cambridge/>** and the e-mail number is <colc@cambridge.gov.uk>

The address for further information is Cambridge Online City, Hobson House, 44 St Andrew's Street, Cambridge CB2 3AS, UK; tel/fax: +44 (0)1223 457999.

10
Geographic experience: confluence
Developing partnerships to empower the local community

ELENORE FISHER

Introduction to Rotherham

The Metropolitan Borough of Rotherham is situated at the confluence of the rivers Don and Rother. It covers 305 sq km, three quarters of which is rural. Built on an industrial past, some parts of the borough are still recovering from the loss of the traditional mining and steel industries. The communities within Rotherham are disparate, with in some cases a very strong sense of community identity. This identity often does not follow any political or geographical boundaries, but may relate to a few streets, neighbouring villages or quite a large rural area. The town centre is a mixture of retail, open areas, the civic centre and housing, with some of the more deprived areas of the town bordering its centre.

The use of information technology in library and information services

Information technology has been an enormous catalyst for change within the library service in Rotherham, enabling us to change what we do, how we do it and where we do it from. It continues to facilitate communication and partnership with local communities. Staff have had to develop new skills and procedures, ways of introducing new systems and bringing together existing systems, services and personnel to work in new and different ways. It has led to change in the way we provide services and in the expectations of our communities – giving managers the challenge of accepting and implementing new procedures and policies whilst not devaluing the essential and traditional information and people skills possessed by the staff.

Rotherham Library and Information Services have for some time been committed to the use of information technology in developing an efficient and effective service for the local communities. The gathering, storage and delivery of public and community information specifically continues to be facilitated by the innovative use of technology where relevant and appropriate. Community information is not a neat package which can be delivered in isolation. By its very nature, if it is to be developed and used most effectively, then cooperation, involvement and commitment are needed.

Current projects and initiatives

A number of initiatives underway in Rotherham Library and Information Services serve to illustrate both the problems and the opportunities encountered when developing effective community information services.

In common with a number of other public library systems, Rotherham has undergone a period of rapid change and restructuring, both of staff and services. We have taken this opportunity to bring together all our information systems – both manual and IT-based – and place them physically within the section of Library and Information Services which is primarily responsible for delivering information to the public, thus creating a direct interface between those who collect, organize and store information and those who deliver it.

To a certain extent, the development of IT-based systems has mirrored that of traditional paper-based systems: we gather information in via a network of community points, and organize, collate and distribute via a range of outlets.

Rotherview

The first major system to be developed, from about 1988, was Rotherview, using viewdata technology and accessed via a network of public terminals. This was initially implemented using Urban

Programme funding (a forerunner to the Single Regeneration Budget described later in this chapter) and its original remit was based on regenerating the local economy. Therefore the information it contained was biased towards the economy and employment; access to job vacancies has always been the most heavily used section. Subjects covered have expanded to include tourist information, education etc. Rotherview continues to develop and it currently forms the core of the local authority website.

In the early 1990s this information was complemented by the development of a 'sister' database of information covering community and voluntary-sector groups, societies, speakers, halls for hire, churches etc. As this has developed, we have streamlined the two services to ensure that we avoid duplication of effort in gathering and storing information. Information collected in is also used to produce hard-copy directories, which continue to be in heavy demand. These are both subject-based and geographically-based. Community involvement in the geographically-based directories is substantial: libraries and other locally based access points collect information, which is passed to the central section responsible for database management. At the directory production stage, community involvement again is substantial: we have found that, although each directory could usefully contain a standard core set of information, a sense of local identity and relevance is extremely important to ensure local input and ownership.

Internet usage

In the mid-1990s Library and Information Services took the lead on developing Internet usage within Rotherham Metropolitan Borough Council. This development has been threefold. Firstly, we have attempted to assess the uses of the Internet as a staff tool, looking at the quality and content of information available. Secondly, we are involved in a rolling programme of offering Internet access at all libraries, as a source of information provided directly to the public. Thirdly, we are using the Internet as a means of publishing information for, about and by a community.

Publishing of information via the Internet encompasses not only joint responsibility for the development of the Rotherham

Metropolitan Borough Council website, but also a specific project managed by Library and Information Services: an electronic local community magazine.

The management and development of this project has forced us to look closely at our aims and strategies, and pointed the way to the future direction and development of a number of our services. It also serves as an example of a project devised at a time when experience of putting the theory into practice was limited, to say the least. The reality may yet turn out to be quite different from the original concept

The project, funded from the Single Regeneration Budget*, is based round the development of an electronic local community magazine serving an area close to the town centre: Eastwood and Oakhill. Internet/intranet technologies enable local editors to create a web-based magazine, distributed both within the local community via a network of public-access terminals sited in appropriate locations, and also over the Internet.[1]

The Eastwood/Oakhill area is a heavily populated, relatively economically deprived area of Rotherham, with a mixture of ethnic populations. The development of the area has formed the basis of a large number of Single Regeneration Budget projects all aimed at regenerating the community. Problems raised by residents include inadequate housing, security, and lack of career prospects and training. With these feelings of dissatisfaction and alienation as a background, it is not surprising that lack of access to information may not be identified within the area as a first priority. However, a community information-based project in this context is not a theoretical abstract, it is one of the means to enable the development and growth of the community.

The project is managed by a member of staff recruited from within the project's geographical area. This has proved to be vital in enabling an effective consultation process with local groups and individuals. It

---

*Single Regeneration Budget funding began in the early 1990s, as a series of annual challenge bids funded directly by the Department of the Environment. Agencies within an area of deprivation are able to bid for funding. Rotherham has been successful in rounds 1–4 inclusive; a bid for round 5 is currently being developed. Agencies wishing to bid for funding under the Single Regeneration Budget should initially contact the economic development section of their local authority for further information.

has been stressed throughout the development of the magazine that it should not be a service provided by 'the Council' for the community: the Library and Information Service is providing the technology and training to enable the community to provide the service *for itself*. A growing network of local editors is encouraging the local community to participate in and own the magazine, and the access points are being located in areas already shown to be natural gathering points. (This has not been without its practical problems: when large areas of housing are being demolished and residents temporarily rehoused, just where do you site a public access point?)

The project manager is also responsible for another Single Regeneration Budget funded project – Gateways to Knowledge – which is intended to provide public access to IT facilities – word processing, CD-ROMs etc – based at locations within the same geographic area. The links between the two projects have proven to be extremely useful: the editors of the magazine are representatives of the local community, with initially an extremely wide range of IT literacy – from someone who had never used a computer before, to professionals working in an IT environment. Access to IT facilities, training and shared experience has brought the two projects closer together, adding extra value to both.

The magazine itself is made up broadly of two sections: that created by the community itself, edited on a number of local terminals; supplemented with access to the already well-established Rotherview service, which provides, for example, information on job vacancies, education and training opportunities. For the last decade, this has been a viewdata-based service, well developed and well used. However, the skills staff have developed in 'translating' this service into one accessible using the Internet have contributed to plans to move away from the viewdata format into a solely Internet-based service. The editors, in consultation and partnership with the wider community, are responsible for deciding what should be included within the magazine. As the project develops, this will give us useful insights into the relative importance of different strands and themes of information, and whether these change as the community develops.

Developing new skills

It has been necessary to develop new and transferable IT skills among staff and within the community – for example, in the installation of the networked public-access terminals, website creation, effective hardware and software security management – which have encouraged the development of relationships between previously separate areas of Library and Information Services, and also with other council areas, eg technical support and telecommunications. This can only help in the consideration of future projects.

The project is seen as a pilot: the core service may be developed in a similar manner within other areas, then focused in on differing community needs.

RAIN

Library and Information Services are also involved in the RAIN project (Rotherham Advice and Information Network). This project, currently under development, aims to use technology to facilitate the provision of effective advice and information services within Rotherham. It proposes to follow a 'hub and spoke' design, consisting of both a major new building within the town centre and a network of outlying agencies and access points. The central building will house a number of agencies, along with training facilities, IT access etc. The IT network has already begun to facilitate improved IT skills and training within the advice and information providers and the setting-up of community access points to a body of community-based information. The IT network will be most effective as it mirrors, and is based on, the strong existing people-based networks already established amongst agencies and within the community – developing partnerships with other bodies to achieve common goals and empowerment.

Public information strategy

The management of information within Library and Information Services is guided by Rotherham MBC's public information strategy. The working group developing the strategy has been chaired by the Head of Service of Library and Information Services, with the involvement, cooperation and backing of a number of other service areas, most notably that responsible for regenerating local communities. The strategy is seen as an efficiency tool and as a means of bringing about more effective corporate working.

Part of the vision statement reads as follows:

> Information is collected without unnecessary duplication, is stored in an appropriate format, and on as open a basis as possible, shared throughout the service areas as widely as possible and disseminated to our customers using appropriate formats and locations. Public information provided by RMBC is of the highest quality in terms of content, delivery and relevance to the needs of both internal and external customers, ensuring an efficient and effective service for all. All staff know and exercise their responsibilities towards public information[2]

If we look at the main areas identified in the management of information – information gathering, storage, sharing and delivery – it may be useful to identify partnerships and changes in work practices which have enabled the improved management of the service.

The gathering of information from the community by Library and Information Services has become more sophisticated with the introduction of new forms of technology – from response frames on Rotherview to feedback gathered from the website (rotherham.gov.uk) to the transfer of data from other council systems – eg the A–Z of Council Services. This has happened against a background of continued strong and developing links with individuals and groups within communities made by individual service points – libraries, community resource centres, council offices. The storage of information has been developed and facilitated by improved use of information technology. We have, where possible, merged and combined data to give greater flexibility and efficiency. In this, it has been important to develop working partnerships with internal RMBC technical-support sections, with outside suppliers and with other local agencies, ensuring that we are progressing in mutually compatible directions.

By sharing information amongst ourselves within libraries, between ourselves and other services and with outside agencies (eg the health authority), it has been possible to reduce duplication, identify gaps in provision and offer shared experience leading to agreed recommended practices.

It is in the delivery of information to the community that the use of IT has perhaps to be handled most sensitively. At times the temptation could have been to forge ahead with the use of IT and leave behind more traditional formats. However, we have attempted to make best use of all appropriate formats – from the World Wide Web, via viewdata, to printed directories, leaflets, telephone and face to face contact. Each one of these will be more appropriate in a given situation than others – technology used to support and enable, not as an end in itself.

Information for a networked community

Any community is a collection of individuals, with both generic and specific information needs. Some communities may appear to be more effective users of information than others, may be more vocal in their demands for information or more directed in its use. But we have all been in the situation where the sudden, unexpected need for specific information usually in a stressful situation such as following a bereavement, redundancy, failing an exam etc – forces us to look again at where we naturally turn to for information. That *may* be to an official body, an advice centre, or a neighbour, parent or friend – and in this the library service may be an official, formal conduit supporting the informal sharing of information. To develop our services most usefully, we need to be aware of these natural sources of information within communities.

Community information is not delivered as a one-way process. Our role is both to provide communities and individuals with access to information and to encourage the active participation of the community in the provision of information, supporting social inclusion and local democracy. In all cases, it is the strong links and partnerships with the community which enable our service to be developed in the most appropriate way.

It may only be a matter of semantics, but we have come to see the difference in emphasis between networked community information (information for, but not necessarily created by, the community) and a community information network. The difference lies in the extent to which the community, however that is defined, is involved in the processes of information gathering and dissemination, thus gaining a genuine sense of ownership and partnership.

References

1   <http:www.rotherham.gov.uk/ecm>
2   Rotherham Metropolitan Borough Council. Library and Information Services, *Public Information Strategy*, November 1997.

11

Locality model
Handsworth Electronic Community Network (HECNet)

GRAHAM BAGSHAW

Introduction

The author first became aware of electronic community networks during a conference in the US in 1991, when an associate from Carleton University in Canada presented a paper on the Canadian National Capital Freenet. This is a system which allows access from computers and terminals in homes and public places to a central computer that holds information of interest to the community (information about schools, colleges, government, libraries and so on), and which facilitates electronic communications between members of the community.

In 1991 this was a new and exciting development in the use of computers and networks, and so, back in the UK, the author discussed with associates Sheila Pantry and David Miller the possibility of similar developments here. Out of these discussions was born the South Yorkshire Network, and the UK Community Information Network conferences in the summers of 1996 and 1997 (CIN '96 and CIN '97). As a result, following CIN '97, the possibility of building an electronic community network for the home locality, Handsworth, began to take shape. Handsworth is a suburb of the City of Sheffield in the county of South Yorkshire. Since then considerable progress has been made. The project has acquired the name Handsworth Electronic Community Network or HECNet.

The nature of Handsworth

Handsworth lies about five miles to the south-east of Sheffield city centre and spans the link road between the city and the main motorway in the UK, the M1. The main road in Handsworth is the old A57 to Worksop, which passes through its centre.

Handsworth is a mixture of old and new. It was recorded in the Domesday Book survey in 1086, and its name is derived from the Anglo-Saxon meaning 'the land enclosed around Hands farmhouse'. St Mary's Parish Church, which stands close to the main road at the highest point in Handsworth, dates from 1170, and its spire can be seen from many miles away in most directions. Handsworth has a link with the US, in that one its inhabitants, a Quaker called Mahlon Stayce, emigrated with his family to America in the 1670s and set up the town of Trenton, which has since become the capital city of the state of New Jersey.

The centre of Handsworth, near to the parish church, consists mainly of stone-built property which dates from the early 1900s and before. The small shops in this area contribute significantly to a village atmosphere, but, as in many other places in the UK, their continued existence is threatened by shopping malls and superstores, one of which is within walking distance.

However, Handsworth consists mainly of housing developments which date from the 1940s to the present. Its population is estimated to be about 15,000, and is fairly mixed in terms of age, wealth, employ-ment status and so on. Unlike some other parts of Sheffield, it does not have any real pockets or concentrations of types of people, and its prob-lems are typical of an area of its nature but are not extreme. During recent years, some difficulties have been introduced by fairly severe reductions in public funding from the local authority. For example, the closure of the Handsworth Branch of the City Library in 1996 came as a great disappointment to many in the community.

Handsworth also accommodates a significant number of business in addition to the small shops: a hypermarket, service businesses and small manufacturing firms.

There is a considerable amount of community activity in Handsworth: it has, for example, four churches, a parish centre which belongs to St Mary's Church, a community centre, a photographic soci-ety, a Cub and a Scout troop, a community nursery, a community library, a historical society, an operatic society, a brass band and, last, but not least, the Handsworth Community Forum.

Initial HECNet developments

It was clear from the outset that to set up an electronic community network would be a large undertaking. This is not something that can be imposed on a community: the community would need to believe that it needed and wanted such a thing in order for the network to stand any chance of success. Therefore, before any serious thought was given to such practical and difficult issues as funding, it was necessary to seek a view from the community. The first question was 'What in Handsworth represents the community?' To seek guidance on this, a meeting was held with the Rector of Handsworth, the Revd Ian Hollin, who was supportive of the project, and recommended that the Handsworth Community Forum (HCF) would be the best place to start. Although the author had lived in Handsworth for several years, he had never even heard of HCF, and was amazed to find this group of enthusiasts, cochaired by Guy de Rouffignac and Janet Hilbert, which was, with very little funding, attempting to look after the community's interests. HCF was founded in 1981, meets every two months, and is attended by representatives of a good cross-section of the community: residents, city councillors, the police, the schools, members of the churches and so on.

As a result of a meeting with Guy de Rouffignac in August 1997, and subsequent discussions, the author gave an initial presentation about the HECNet proposal to the HCF in October 1997. He had anticipated, and this was confirmed at this meeting, that the major difficulty in making such a proposal is that it is in the main impossible to explain what is proposed, simply because the average person still has had little practical exposure to the technologies which would be required. It seemed therefore that what was needed was a demonstration. So, with the help of a couple of volunteers, the author set about building a World Wide Web site[1] which could be used both to give members of HCF a demonstration of what could be provided electronically in terms of local, national and global information, and to give them some hands-on experience. In achieving this, it was fortunate that among the members of the HCF is Martin Bell, Deputy Head of the Handsworth

Grange School, who offered the use of the school's IT facilities for the demonstration. With the enthusiastic help of the school's Head of IT, Ian Footit, and his colleagues, a successful demonstration was given to the Forum on 22 April 1998. The demonstration achieved its objectives in showing Forum members what might be possible, and it also showed them that this 'modern technology' is neither difficult nor frightening to use: indeed, a couple of members were 'converted' from their previous scepticism about the Internet.

Proposed facilities

The term 'electronic community network' is being used to describe the Handsworth proposal, but there are alternative names – for example, freenets, community networks and community information networks – all of which are approximately equivalent. There is no precise definition of any of these terms, but workers in the field have described different models. For the Handsworth proposal, the word 'community' is intended to cover all individuals and groups who live and work in the area, and includes businesses.

The vision is that HECNet will provide the following for the community:

- a wide source of local, national, and global information
- a means for local businesses and community organizations to market and advertise their services and products, locally and worldwide
- a facility for fast, efficient and cost-effective communications between individuals and between groups
- a means to improve information, communications and IT skills in general
- a new environment which will empower and engender creativity.

It is expected that, for the foreseeable future, the technological basis for this proposal will be the Internet – in particular, the World Wide Web, electronic mail and electronic mailing lists.

At present, one of the biggest stumbling blocks for projects of this type is the problem of providing access to the community network. A short survey carried out by a Handsworth school a few months ago showed that only a small percentage of the community had access to the Internet from home. The IT Industry envisages that, in a few years' time, access to the Web will be provided much more widely than at present – for example, by means of interactive television. In the mean-time, access can be improved by providing public access points, but these are expensive and constrain the value of the network because people have to travel to use them. One way to limit such constraints is to provide public access in places that people visit frequently, regularly and as a matter of course – for example, in the entrance of a superstore.

The pilot study

Building an electronic community network would clearly be a large undertaking: even setting up the demonstration website took several weeks of effort. This is not an undertaking that the HCF is ready to adopt, and perhaps more importantly, the need in the Handsworth community has not yet been established. Therefore, in March 1998 with guidance from the Sheffield Training and Enterprise Council (TEC), the HCF agreed to carry out a survey to determine whether the community both needs and wants such a network. At the time of writing, this project is under way.

It was decided that, with a population of 15,000 or so, about 500 or so individuals should be interviewed so that a fair picture could be gained. This sample is to come from householders, businesses, community organizations, societies and so on. The work required is considerable, and it was therefore decided to apply for funding from European Social Fund (ESF), Objective 3, Priority 4, which is concerned with the capacity-building of communities. Because the HCF had no experience of bidding for such funding, the Sheffield TEC undertook to be the applicant, with HCF as the main beneficiary. While the meat of the work is the survey, from an ESF point of view the project will facilitate training and skills in research, IT, finance and business for up to 16 members of the community. This will provide new skills and employment opportunities for some unemployed people in the community, and will give the HCF the basic skills needed to bid and manage funding for community projects in the future.

Approval for the ESF funding was obtained in late July 1998, and expenditure completed by the end of December. This imposed a fairly tight timetable on the survey.

The main purpose of the survey is to obtain a measure of whether an electronic community network would be viable. However, it is not possible to ask a simple question about the need, since typical interviewees will not be aware of the concept, nor will they have had any experience of the underlying technology. So the basic approach that is being taken in the questionnaire is to ask about information and communication needs, how well these are currently satisfied, and how a new and better facility would appeal. At the same time, the opportunity is being taken to carry out an audit of IT facilities and skills in the community.

Twelve local unemployed people were recruited as interviewers during September 1998. In early October they were trained by professional workers in interviewing skills, in survey-specific skills and in the IT skills needed to enable them to enter the collected data into a survey-analysis package. Interviewing started in mid-October, and over 400 interviews have been completed.

Interviews are prearranged, are conduced in people's homes, etc, and the interviewer works through and completes a standard questionnaire which was designed as part of the project with help from the Sheffield TEC and the University of Sheffield's Department of Sociological Studies. After completing a batch of interviews, the interviewer keys the results into a survey-analysis package at Handsworth Grange School. When they are returned, a fixed payment is made per questionnaire. Thus interviewers take responsibilily for, and claim ownership of, the questionnaires throughout the process, arranging the interview, carrying it out and entering the data.

During December 1998, the results of the survey were analysed using the survey-analysis package, and a report is being written. This will include an initial business plan for the development of an electronic community network, if the need is proven.

The next stage

The future of HECNet will be strongly influenced by the outcome of the survey. If the survey shows a significant need, HCF will be guided by the business plan. An essential element will be funding, the need for which is likely to be considerable. However, the skills provided to the HCF by the current ESF project will help with the development of suitable bids for the funds needed to put the network in place. But once it has been set up, a big issue for the future will be how to sustain the network in the long term. Possible sources of long-term income are sponsorship from businesses, Web design work and ICT training facilities.

If the survey shows only a small need, the position will have to be reconsidered, and perhaps reviewed after a year or two. In any event, the author expects that the website (the informational aspect of the network) would continue to be developed on a voluntary basis, if only at a relatively low level. A by-product of the work so far is that individuals who have the necessary interest, enthusiasm and skills to do the necessary work, are beginning to emerge from the community.

Observations

In summary, the following observations, whilst they relate specifically to Handsworth, are probably typical:

1   A lot of activity in the community is hidden from public view: individuals and groups work hard for the good of the community, often without marketing their activities. The Handsworth Community Forum is an example of this.

2   Despite all the general talk in the media about computers, IT, ICT, the Internet and so on, general awareness in the community remains fairly low.

3   This is a constraint on the introduction of an electronic network since the concept is new to most people.

4   However, if people are given the opportunity to see and try out the technology, they typically come to grips with the basic concepts quickly, and can see its potential for the community.

5   Even though general IT awareness is limited, there are significant pockets of resources of this type which, when identified, could be of considerable benefit to ICT-based projects like HECNet and to the community in general.

6   Setting up an electronic community network would be a big and relatively expensive task, requiring considerable initial and ongoing funding.

7   Even setting up a pilot scheme for evaluation purposes has involved a considerable amount of time and effort, which has needed external funding.

8   Last but not least, the project has already shown that there is a considerable amount of latent capability within the community. Almost all the interviewers in the survey have had no previous experience of this type of work, and yet, following professional training, within a very short time most of them are performing well in this new and skilful work.

Conclusions

Setting up an electronic community network has to be a bottom–up process, the community has first to feel a strong need before it can commit to the considerable resources that are needed. Given the present limited awareness and access to the required technology, this will inevitably be a slow process. Nevertheless, over the last year, the Community Forum's reaction to the proposal for a network in Handsworth has been positive, encouraging and supportive. The present ESF-funded survey should give a much better feel for the general need in households, businesses and community organizations. Hopefully, this will lead to a firm proposal and business plan for a network. Funding the development and maintenance of this network will be a major issue, but the training given to the Forum by the current ESF project should provide the skills and information needed to realize this.

The ESF fund is concerned with capacity-building in the community. The project has already started to achieved this: 12 previously unemployed people have increased their skills, confidence and employment potential, and as a direct result of the project, one of these people has already been offered employment in market research as from the beginning of January 1999. It has become abundantly clear that the community in general possesses great potential to improve its level of activity, skills and effectiveness.

References

1   <http://www.handsworth.org.uk>

12

Subject model
Networks for learning

SHEENA BANKS

Lifelong learning and CINs

The development of community information networks (CINs) and the important role they have in building capacity and awareness of information and communications technology (ICT) in local communities, is having a major impact on access to lifelong learning.

The use of ICT within lifelong learning with access facilitated by local networks and centres can not only overcome physical barriers of time, place and distance, but also give lifelong learners greater independence and flexibility in what they choose to learn. The participation of individuals in CINs provides a new capacity for education and training, particularly in the development of skills and competence for using ICT, which can effectively meet the needs of individual learners. The same technologies which support the development of CINs also support the growth of local learning centres. However, the use of ICT in learning also presents new issues of access which must be overcome for learners in the community to participate fully in 'the information society'. Field[1] observes that new technology is 'changing the educational landscape' but highlights the need for a strategic inclusive approach to ICT literacy. This is an essential prerequisite for access to learning via ICT.

In the UK the use of ICT in lifelong learning is now seen as a strategic imperative that is both educationally and economically important. However, much of the national policy debate has been driven by the potential of technology itself rather than by a vision of innovation in learning delivered via the technology. Implementation of the National Grid for Learning is now underway, albeit focused in the schools sector, and there are further developments following publication of the Government's Green Paper *The Learning Age*.[2] The University for Industry has now been created and developments are underway via a number of major projects. The University for Industry is a learning network which will make use of the National Learning Grid to make learning more accessible to adult learners in the community and in the workplace, and will provide online information and guidance. There is an assumption in these developments that the implementation of physical connectivity and the creation of local learning centres will in themselves achieve wider access and participation in learning, while as yet there is no indication as to how demand for online learning will be created. Connectivity needs, access to local learning centres, and local capacity for sustaining them, vary widely, often because of circumstances of geography and existing capacity. As yet there are no national benchmarks for standards of facilities and provision.

The networked learning environment and its significance for access

Access to learning through ICT requires the development of a distributed learning environment through Internet technology – learners being linked through the Internet at a variety of venues, and accessing Internet tools and technologies for communication and learning.

During the period 1996–98 the University of Sheffield developed a networked learning infrastructure as part of the economic regeneration of the Dearne Valley. The Dearne Valley is a former coalfield area in South Yorkshire which continues to experience social and economic disadvantage following major industrial demise. The networked infrastructure developed links from the main campus of the University to an HE Centre in the new Dearne Valley College, to other further education colleges in the area and to local community centres, libraries and schools within the wider community. The Dearne Valley Project was funded by £2 million from the Coalfields Strategic Projects Fund and its first phase described here was completed in March 1998.

The project implemented a networked learning infrastructure as part of certain economic regeneration strategies in the Dearne Valley which led in 1995 to the building of the new Dearne Valley (FE) College on former coalfield land in the Dearne Valley, surrounded by a large enterprise zone. The University of Sheffield formed a partnership with the Dearne Valley College and two other local colleges with a view to collectively enhancing higher education opportunities and collaborating on the development of a networked learning infrastructure and learning environment to improve access to both FE and HE in the area. The collaboration also included working with schools, adult educators, libraries and community centres in the area to begin to establish learning pathways.

Key developments in the project have included the building of an HE centre at the Dearne Valley College, telematically linked to the main campus of Sheffield University, to other FE colleges in South Yorkshire, and to some schools, community centres and libraries in the local area.

The underpinning philosophy of these developments was the belief that the creation of an ICT infrastructure with local access can overcome barriers of time and place, offer both basic and high-level skills and knowledge, foster learning in regional and local contexts, and in this respect ameliorate social and economic exclusion. The ICT infrastructure also has a major impact on economic regeneration by creating facilities which contribute both to inward investment and to new opportunities for building a local skilled and qualified workforce, and which boost the capability of local business to compete in global markets.

Designing for distributed access

The project has created a local technology infrastructure as a means of delivering and supporting FE and HE courses which will allow local people to take advantage of courses without leaving the area. This has been achieved by extending the University LAN through a 2-megabyte Ethernet link to the HE Centre at the Dearne Valley College, and then by extending this to other centres to create the infrastructure. Technical support was provided from Sheffield. Internet tools, technologies and groupware were developed through this network.

These links were then extended via Internet connections into the community to a range of community venues – schools, libraries and community centres. These community partners have been supported during the project in the development of these resources as community information networks to spread out the impact into the wider community.

The ICT technology developed provides electronic links via the University, the Dearne Valley College, the other colleges and community venues for the wider community, for access to HE and FE courses, and library, careers and student support facilities, enabling learners to access resources locally and to be supported online. A virtual university trial in the project has been used to examine ways in which networked learning can be used to support the cost-effective provision of quality education and training in this 'distributed' community. This trial has been used to evaluate various groupware through user trials and other issues to provide cost-effective learner support. The groupware has included LotusNotes, First Class and Microsoft Exchange. This virtual university concept developed considers how to support online all aspects of a traditional campus-based university learning programme – including library services, careers and guidance, learning support, assessment and administration – for the benefit of off-campus learners.

Developing the learning environment

The project has considered the requirements needed for a learning environment, which effectively supports online learners. The model shown in Figure 12.1 was developed for the project by McConnell.[3] It brings together the elements required for effective online learning and shows how learning can be distributed to a wider community for learners who may be in another institution, at work, in a community setting or at home. Evaluation of the learner groups in the project shows that this learning environment can support effective online learning. The use of LotusNotes groupware, for example, has been particularly successful. Access to learning through ICT requires the development of a *distributed* learning environment through Internet technology, learners being linked through the Internet at a variety of venues and accessing Internet tools and technologies for communication and learning. The

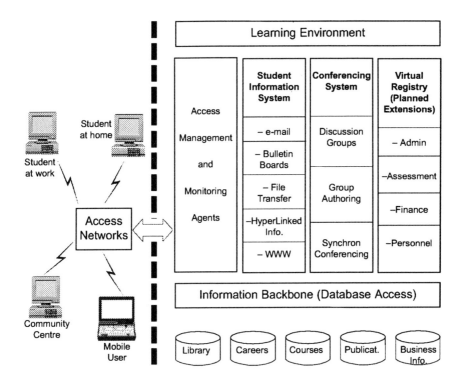

Fig. 12.1   *Support System (DV Intranet)*

learning pedagogy being developed is computer-supported collaborative learning (CSCL) – forms of learning which support collaborative
and social processes. The project has supported the development of a
community Internet through an ISP connectivity and modem access
through public telephone lines. This same technology is being used to
link in to users at home and in the workplace. For example, many of
the teachers associated with the project are connected both at home and
at their place of work. Key users have been provided with an ISP link
giving them a local point-of-presence (PoP) and Internet access at local
rate, a 28.8 kb/s MultiTech modem and in some cases a PC. The focus
on the 'distributed community' links has meant close liaison with
schools, libraries and community groups within the area. This has been
to foster 'community ownership' of the ICT capability which is developing.

   These developments are now being incorporated into a sub-regional
infrastructure involving all colleges, TECs and universities in South

Yorkshire, including Distributed Centres of Excellence and a South Yorkshire University for Industry project. They are being enhanced by transnational partnership to develop virtual learning in a European context and working to European standards of online learner competence. However, there are concerns that the regional ICT infrastructure developments are not providing consistent levels of access, particularly in non-urban areas, and that many communities are being further disadvantaged by lack of access to ICT facilities.

Converging CINs with networked learning

It is essential that all user groups in a community – the local adult population, young people, education users such as schools, business, industry and community and voluntary organizations – should be catered for in the provision of Internet technology in a form which is affordable and sustainable. A multi-user base for the facilities developed is essential. The varied needs and 'agendas' of local users can be incorporated into ICT facilities which combine the use of the Internet for learning with community access via a distributed system which can also be used for community information networks. With the emergence of community and voluntary sectors as contributors to regeneration and capacity building in their own right, the multi-agency ICT facility can be an integral part of economic and social regeneration. Hoogvelt and Freeman,[4] in discussing the potential for community intranets and the participation of the socially excluded, commented that 'a local (developing into a municipal) network would vastly increase the opportunities for local agents to be participants in local economic hubs that are competitive in the world economy as well'.

This means multi-agency collaboration for the development of ICT facilities which meet local and global needs and are affordable to all. Normann et al[5] argue that segmentation of different sectors 'flies in the face of what is today known as a new logic of value creation in which added value is created not in sequential chains, but rather in complex value constellations'. So both the development of ICT capability and its use as either a community information network or a learning centre, must be the responsibility of key stakeholders working together and seeking to implement new and innovative applications.

The impact of ICT in lifelong learning is changing the terms of reference for educational delivery and production, and giving rise to new ideas about access to learning and how learning accessed via ICT can impact on the wider community – extending the resources of institutions beyond their boundaries. The key features of networked learning are

- the opportunity to organize and manipulate learning content to meet the needs of individual learners
- the capacity to communicate with other learners.

Computer-supported collaborative learning (CSCL) has already been proved to be successful as a learning medium which facilitates networked learning. CSCL promotes cooperative and group learning which provides a context where the learners 'can take control of their own learning in a social context'.[6] This means that ICT can stimulate the development of individual, group and experiential learning, rather than just the acquisition of 'knowledge' which is taught. This means that the development of access to learning via ICT will incorporate individual, group and community knowledge alongside formal knowledge. It has been found that learners can create close and supportive relationships in the online learning community. This online community spirit has been identified by Sproull and Kiesler,[7] who suggest that 'open access networks favour the free flow of information . . . and lead to a kind of electronic altriuism quite different from the fears that networks would weaken the social fabric of organizations'. It is accepted that the concept of the learning community can be incorporated into the online environment and have benefits for real communities.

This may mean extending the idea of community from 'having a geographical local focus to being a community of interests'.[8] This has a real significance for community information networks that can be extended both locally and globally. It also has strategic significance for lifelong learning.

References

1   Field, J, The adult learner as listener, viewer and cybersurfer, *Electronic*

pathways: adult learning and the new communication technologies, NIACE, 1997.

2   Department for Education and Employment, *The learning age* (Green Paper), TSO, 1998.

3   McConnell, D, *Networked learning support system* (Dearne Valley Project Report), University of Sheffield. 1996.

4   Hoogvelt, A and Freeman, M, *Community intranets* (Executive Summary from BT Research Report), 1996.

5   Normann, R and others, From value chain to value constellation: designing interactive strategy, *Harvard business review*, July–August 1993, 65–77.

6   McConnell, D, *Implementing computer supported cooperative learning*, Kogan Page, 1994.

7   Sproull, L and Kiesler, S, Computers, networks and work, *Scientific American*, **265** (3), 1991, 84–91.

8   Rheingold, H, Virtual communities. In *Computer conferencing: the last word*, Beach Holme Publishers, 1992.

13

Specific groups model
Women Connect: using and shaping the Internet together – women getting online and connected

MARION SCOTT AND MARGARET PAGE

Genesis of an idea

The UK women's sector is vibrant despite having to work under considerable pressures, including significant reductions in available funding. The sector includes all kinds of not-for-profit organizations, community and voluntary groups, professional organizations and self help groups. In particular, it provides a huge range of services, most of which are unique and vital for the well-being of millions of women. As well as all this, it enables women to voice their opinions and helps to create an informed constituency – so important for democracy and for a disadvantaged and diverse group such as women.

The idea of Women Connect was a practical response to the networking and resourcing needs of women's organizations. The starting point was the nature of the sector and its challenges – networking and information help us to are essential to learn, to lobby, to strengthen and support and share, and to promote. The stimulus and desire to develop the idea arose itself out of women networking – linking up as individuals and through their work in organizations.

The Internet appeared even on the surface to offer potential to meet some of the needs – for shared information resources and for networking – critical for the effectiveness of women's organizations. By the mid-1990s the new information and communication technology of the Internet was emerging into much wider use. It was clearly here to stay. There were publications about the progressive and community-based uses of the Internet in the US and elsewhere. The United Nations' Fourth World Conference on Women in Beijing in 1995 vividly demonstrated its value for non-governmental organization (NGO) lobbying, communication and collaboration in a progressive context. An Internet event run by the Women's Computer Centre (no longer funded) in London was a further catalyst.

Marion Scott and Margaret Page started a joint piece of development and research to work up the project in early 1997. They were helped in this developmental work and the early stages by GreenNet – the UK-based ISP, part of the Association of Progressive Communicators (APC) international network. The APC women's programme has a strong focus on the developing world, and their survey of the take-up of the Internet by women's organizations was an inspiring report confirming the relevance of the concept. The Community Development Foundation (CDF) – familiar with, and active in, other strands of electronic community networking – took up the proposal because of their experience of working on community-related information and communication technology (ICT) issues and social inclusion, and also their perception of the need to strengthen the use of online communications by women at local level through a practical innovative project. An application in spring 1997 to the National Lottery Charities Board was successful. The Library Association then joined the consortium, bringing specialist knowledge of the information society and extensive contacts in the library network.

Our mission

Women Connect aims to use the Internet, and a commitment to learning and networking across different areas of experience and expertise, to build a sustainable community of women's organizations and resource contacts who are working in diverse communities and fields. We set out to enable women's organizations to use and shape the Internet to benefit women. The project supports, advises, trains and equips member organizations to develop skills in using the Internet and networking – for communication, information, visibility, collaboration and learning. As a result, members have the potential to improve their practice and innovate, grasp opportunities, form partnerships, access wider resources, influence decision-makers and widen their impact – using the Internet together to meet their organizational objectives for women. Women Connect links with other projects to build an online presence that is of value to women in the UK and beyond – shaping the Net to benefit women. This is illustrated graphically in the wheel diagram in Figure 13.1.

There is a challenge to all of us to work *together* to use the potential of new information and communication technologies. Women Connect aims to build organizational capacity for the future. Women Connect was the first UK-based women's Internet networking project of its kind aiming to strengthen all women's organizations and what they do in their communities.

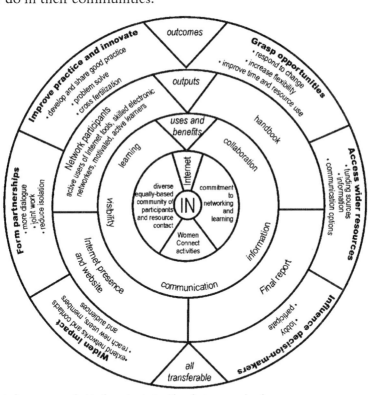

inner circle:	what is there to start with: what we need or have
first ring:	uses and benefits of networking/electronic networking
second ring:	measurable changes
outer ring:	longer term outcomes (changes) for women's organizations within and beyond the initial network

Fig. 13.1   *The structure of Women Connect*

The project's first phase

Women Connect began work in January 1998 to create a sustainable electronic network of women's organizations and resource contacts throughout the regions of England. Following a promotion, information and selection exercise, 20 organizations joined as first-phase project members.

The 20 organizations participating in the first phase of 23 months in 1998–99 are spread throughout the regions of England. What they have in common is an understanding of the value of networking and a wish to explore new ways of communicating and exchanging information, in order to achieve their organizational objectives.

They are a diverse set of grass-roots and larger or national organizations, with very varying levels of experience of using information and communication technologies. The member groups work in a variety of communities, policy, service or campaigning areas. They organizations include national and locally based organizations, refuges, health and advice centres, generic women's training and education organizations, centres, a lesbian project, an older women's organization, some black and minority ethnic women's organizations, local and national networks, groups and organizations run on an unfunded, voluntary basis or with high dependence on volunteer input. Some are collectives, others more traditionally hierarchical.

What we do

The groups come into membership and sign up to an agreement to clarify what the project Women Connect would will provide and what each organization commits to do. An equipment assessment forms the basis for allocating resources from the budget such as computers, modems and telephone lines to some of the organizations. Each receives a subsidy for ISP costs and additional monies to cover some telecommunications bills. The project coordinators work with all the members to draw up a Women Connect action plan for introducing and taking up use of the Internet, tailored to the needs and objectives of the individual organization. When the action plan is formalized, an onsite trainer visits each organization in turn to train a small group, guided by the action plan. She provides feedback to the coordinators on her work. Group events known as development days are held around the country, allowing face-to-face networking to build the network and share learning and experiences of using and shaping the Internet. Group training days are another opportunity to meet and share and learn new skills needed by the whole network. Women Connect contracts with individual trainers and advisors to provide these services. They have also contracted with a training company to deliver website building training with small groups of trainees. Each activity is monitored.

Another part of the experimental design of the project are 'resource contacts'. These are individual women who act as 'voluntary' advisors and join the network. The idea is that they help member organizations to access a range of help, information and contacts. They will include information and communication technology (ICT)/Internet experts, and also practitioners with experience in working on women's issues in particular policy areas or in activities like fundraising or lobbying.

While the training, development and support activities were going on in the first phase <**www.womenconnect.org.uk**> was developed and going live in November 1998. It is designed to evolve as a source of UK-relevant information and links, and discussion about and for women's organizations. It includes pages about each of the member organizations, and gradually more and more links to their own sites as they feel able to develop and maintain them independently. These links and pages and sites are evidence of the growing presence of UK women's organizations shaping and using the net. In the longer term, the site will offer wider discussion opportunities, and links to other sites and areas of communication and collaboration such as newsgroups and mailing/discussion lists of interest to women's organizations in the UK.

Also, in late 1998, an invitation-only web-based discussion board started work – an electronic space for members' collaboration, learning and exchange – free to the project because it was set up through a commercial site on a trial basis. All member organizations are invited to participate, and also trainers, selected project advisors, resource contacts and others. Two months later about third of the organizations were regular users.

The website, publications, and a conference in late 1999, are ways of sharing the learning and resources arising from Women Connect's work with the wider community, especially women's organizations. Women Connect is creating a sustainable, transferable set of working practices that can be adapted for use by others. Members take part in the evaluation of the project's work and the dissemination of results. Online material and a handbook for wider use within UK-based community networks, targeted especially at women's organizations, are in production.

Equality issues

Women Connect's mission is to build a sustainable community of women's organizations and resource contacts who are working in diverse communities and fields. Women Connect's approach to equalities has sought seeks to acknowledge and work with differences of power, and it sets out to address and challenge inequality, while drawing on diversity.

Women Connect member organizations are diverse but have all stated a commitment to equality. From the start organizations run by black and minority ethnic women, older women and lesbians became involved. There are organizations working with other groups of women – for instance, disabled women, women on low pay, refugees and asylum seekers.

An equalities perspective and the use of good practice is applied to the range of processes and content within the development and delivery of the project – to service delivery and subcontracting, events and on-site visits for training and development, the development of electronic workspaces, recruitment of resource contacts, the development of a web presence, project advice, monitoring and evaluation, the production of materials and reporting to funders.

Women Connect has begun to grapple with the challenge of a mixed network: one hard-pressed service providing minority ethnic group has questioned the direct relevance of the network, looking to use Women Connect as a springboard for creating other networks of organizations with whom they feel they have more in common. Other black and minority ethnic-based groups seem willing to give the 'generic' environment a try. Clearly, as the network grows, special focus groups and regional connections may flourish.

Other learning

The first phase of the project provided much learning.
    In general we found the following:

1 Our key starting assumptions were right – about: the key role of face-to-face networking; the role of on-site visits to sustain motivation and momentum; the need to embed and integrate the use of the Internet within organizational objectives and practice.
2 There is a need to explore the different purposes and values of networking.
3 We need to look at the nature of the technology and how it both shapes and offers opportunities – it is not a neutral tool.
4 The lessons from Women Connect can be examined for the benefit of other communities, including other non locality communities.
5 There is a lack of a UK presence on the Internet in the area of women's organizations, and of materials and spaces for social change relating to women and women's organizations.
6 It is crucial to monitor and evaluate to make case for more resources.
7 Funders of women's initiatives should recognize ICTs as necessary parts of standard organizational infrastructure for effectiveness.
8 Women's initiatives are still sidelined: to make mainstreaming genuine, amongst other things, policy and funders must target resources for ICTs to key communities such as women.
9 Women's organizations need a higher profile to highlight their good practice in delivering services and their contribution to learning about the potential of ICT usage within the community and voluntary sector; women's organizations need to be able to access more resources for ICT and much else.
10 A long-term perspective is appropriate.
11 A variety of partnerships are relevant to further this and related work.

    In terms of the 20 women's organizations, it seems that the programme must take account of

•   considerable flux and change within women's organizations
•   a wide variation in the pace at which individuals and organizations

can absorb new work practices and many levels of ability and commitment
- the timing of activities, which needs to be flexible
- the variety of factors which help/hinder the take-up of opportunities.

In particular we have found the following factors significant:

Shared commitment

Women Connect shares commitment to women with the members.
This is necessary where organizations are working for social change and
on challenging agendas. Support and development programmes/proj-
ects need to know how to respond appropriately to the difficulties of
this environment.

The impact of underresourcing

Women's organizations as a sector are underfunded for the work they do:
funders have confirmed that they undersell and undercost their work.
The impact of lack of resources puts a strain on existing practice and
impedes development. Projects like Women Connect must recognize
this. Our approach, focused on organizational development, ultimately
seeks to enable groups themselves to address this fundamental problem of
resourcing.

Pace

Where organizations are working over capacity, additional activities
sometimes need to be introduced at a slow and variable pace. We have
looked at whether and when this changes, and what is needed to sustain momentum.

Changes

A large proportion of the member organizations have experienced
some form of change in a 12–18-month period: staff turnover, Women
Connect key worker changes, loss of funding, management changes,

office moves etc. This inevitably impacts on their capacity to develop.

Timescales

The lesson is to devise flexible programmes while achieving adequate momentum and setting some targets.

Equipment

A number of issues are presented during the selection and provision of equipment and it is a time-consuming task. However, without appropriate hardware and software the organizations could not participate effectively. We are now concerned that many organizations need more than one computer linked to the Internet for whole-organization strategies.

Service providers/project management

Service providers working for the Women Connect programme need a combination of skills, experience and commitment that is hard to get and retain. This presents a challenge.

Training and support

This is labour-intensive and costly in time and resources; Women Connect also encourages member organizations to access local low-cost or free training opportunities and ICT support organizations.

Diversity

Women Connect has a diverse membership, across many dimensions – including age, ethnic background of users/staff, management structures, paid or volunteer status, funded and low or unfunded. This has given a unique insight into the range of needs within the sector in relation to using and shaping the Internet and more generally.

Activity rates

It has not always been possible to predict the actual activity levels of individual organizations from their initial statements, application forms and action plans which give a picture of levels of expertise and aspiration – many factors can intervene positively and negatively.

Face to face

The face-to-face events have been inspiring and motivational – despite being difficult to organize and more costly in time and resources.

Levels

Our programmes have to accommodate different levels and paces of learning.

Match

For some organizations, there is an apparently closer match between what the Internet does relatively easily already and what they want to do. For example, an internationally oriented women's network can use a wide range of information and communication options.

Time out /making space

Individuals have found time out away from the distractions of work and worries about online costs beneficial to learning and development.

Whole-organization commitment

Champions and competent users within organizations have sometimes needed help in getting colleagues to take the work on board. Individuals need to find some more personally based motivation to go online and get connected. The whole organization needs to have a commitment. Individual member organizations are developing models of transfer and development of skills.

Resources

There are sometimes hidden skills in organizations: individuals possessing them can help share skills and motivate others.

Multi-tasking

Even where to locate the computer is an issue – deciding who would use the Internet-connected computer for what and when is very central for many members.

Interactive tools

The right community networking Internet tools are not yet so easily accessible, and not always user-friendly: Women Connect is exploring the possibilities and drawing up its own specifications – shaping the Internet.

Some quick hits

New users of the Internet need some easy results: the Women Connect website, the learning community and its electronic workspace, resource contacts and tailored training, are part of the design to get organizations over the initial barriers.

Networking

Face-to-face networking is highly valued by the members, who are increasingly convinced of the potential of electronic networking in all its forms and competent in its usage. During the programmed opportunities for face-to-face networking, member organizations exchange experiences, lessons and ideas on a wide range of matters – how to share ICT skills and raise motivation within organizations, practical suggestions for funding sources, website addresses, 'sistering' schemes. A learning community is in the making – addressing a continuum of issues from basic 'technical/how to' questions to 'what's on the net that's of use to women's organizations', to how to take up and adapt the electronic communication capacities of the technology for women and social change.

Small steps, major changes

Some organizations are very pleased with just getting online – something they do not think would have happened without the stimulus of Women Connect. Others have made significant developments in their ways of working. All can see some benefit for their organization, whether it comes in the longer term or more immediately. As one member put it, after only one year it became possible for the network to 'discuss the Internet and the software using a language that one year ago was alien to many of our ears'.

What next?

Community Development Foundation (CDF) will continue to provide invaluable support to the project in a planned second phase. This will include a progression towards independence in line with CDF's commitment to appropriate management following a period of innovation and development of a new project.

Women Connect plans to develop in three areas working with key players and in particular arenas:

- in women's organizations, women in organizations, networks of women and women's organizations, and women-friendly initiatives, by developing and sustaining their learning to use the Internet to meet their objectives
- in the virtual world, by creating and extending, using and shaping the virtual world to work for women's organizations and women
- in politics and resources (including stakeholders and funders) by informing policy and practice, particularly around women and ICTs, access, resourcing, interactivity, informancy and dialogue.

Women Connect – using and shaping the Internet together!

14

The associations
Communities Online and the European Association for Community Networking

DAVID WILCOX AND MICHAEL MULQUIN

All around the UK are a whole range of exciting and innovative projects that are trying out ways in which the new information and communications technologies can help people find out what is going on in their local communities and get involved themselves. Some of these are local authority initiatives, some are being run by community organizations, some are initiatives of universities and colleges, and some are the result of commercial interests.

The problem is that it is very difficult to find out about all of these initiatives because of the very diversity of their origin. This also means that there is a lot of learning going on around the country both as to what works and to what doesn't. This is information that government, both central and local, needs to know about so that public resources can be used strategically to support the kinds of initiatives that are likely to succeed.

Communities Online was set up to support this growing movement that is putting a human face on the information society.

How did Community Online start?

David Wilcox was the main instigator of Communities Online, and acted as editor and director until early 1998, when Michael Mulquin became executive director.

Communities Online was born and nurtured through chance meetings, the generosity of our American cousins, the support of companies and Government departments, help from an East London charity, and the effort of a lot of pioneers in the field.

The first important chance meeting was at the first Annual Conference of the Urban Forum - then part of the National Council for Voluntary Organizations (NCVO) - in April 1995, when David Wilcox ran a workshop about partnerships, networks and the possible benefits of using the Internet.

He had worked for many years in 'real world' partnerships and had been fired with enthusiasm for the potential of the Net to create 'partnerships for tomorrow' by virtual visits via the Net to community networks and bulletin boards operating in the US.

The US connection

The following month he was due to attend 'The Ties that Bind' a conference organized by the Morino Institute and Apple at the home of Apple Computers in Cupertino, California, which he had spotted on the Web. That was made possible by the first important act of generosity: Steve Cisler, community networking guru at Apple, and Kaye Gapen, of Morino, had responded to a flurry of pleading e-mails from David by waiving fees and paying his fare and hotel. Fundraising on the Net had worked!

After his session at the Urban Forum conference, the greatest coenthusiast was Michael Mulquin, who was then working for the Community Involvement Unit of Aston Charities in Newham, UK. He was to become the most ardent champion of local electronic networking in the UK, initially through his role on the Urban Forum steering group, then as chair of Communities Online and finally as executive director.

Cupertino was amazing – not only as the home of the Macintosh but as the host for a conference filled for three days with several hundred people who weren't just talking about what the Net could for local communities, but were actually doing it. At Cupertino and at subsequent events, David met people like Steve Snow, Terry Grunwald, Philippa Gamse, Amy Borgstrom, Frank Odasz and Doug Schuler, who provided inspiration and encouragement for our efforts in the UK.

UK developments

Over the following months, more activities were already developing in the UK. Many people were thinking the same way, and had already achieved a great deal. Community networking wasn't new in the UK - it just needed networking nationally as well as locally. Chris Studman was starting a network in Coventry; Nick Plant and Morris Williams were working on Community Telematics in Bristol; virtual towns were beginning in Manchester and also Brighton, where David Wilcox lived.

David Fitzpatrick of Computer Access had been there before everyone, helping create Poptel to provide the voluntary sector with Internet access, and working with communities in East London. North of the border, Craigmillar had its own network run by Andy McDonald, and communities in the Highlands and Islands had been using the Internet for direct-dial systems for years to conquer distance. John O'Hara had created the South Bristol Learning Network, later to foster the Cyberskills Association backed by ICL.

Crucially for Communities Online, as it turned out, Richard Stubbs was planning to create a conference for practitioners in community-based regeneration on Compuserve. He too lived in Newham, and had already come across Michael Mulquin in other connections.

Richard decided to join forces, and with Michael and David formed Partnerships for Tomorrow (P4T). We worked to create a demonstration Community Regeneration Network on a FirstClass system called pHreak, run by Intermedia Associates.

Corporate support

At this point another chance meeting, combined with our first corporate support, provided the resources to begin to turn dreams into reality.

The funds came from BT's community affairs department, where Norman Howard was able to make the case to colleagues for supporting the emerging network and a seminar called Communities Online run jointly with Urban Forum at BT Centre in October 1995.

The chance meeting came in a Brighton bookshop, where David's enquiries about publications on the Internet led owner Richard Cupidi to introduce him to BT strategist Dave Greenop, who lived in Hove.

Dave could see how the bottom-up vision of community networking could mesh with some of the commercial scenarios for telecommunications in the information age. He introduced David to fellow-futurist at BT Labs Ian Pearson, and together they hosted a meeting of 30 key people in September 1995. With that and the October seminar at BT Centre, we felt we were on the map.

South Yorkshire network

It was about this time that we discovered that in South Yorkshire Dave Miller, Sheila Pantry and Graham Bagshaw had been working for some time on developing a regional forum for community networkers that would lead to the first Community Information Networks Conference at Sheffield University in 1996.

The September meeting of P4T provided the basis for a steering group led by Michael, and a strategy hacked out in flurry of presentations and post-it notes. It was decided that the role of P4T should be as a network and information system for promoting debate on the impact of new media technologies on communities and exploring their benefits. It was also to act as a referral point for existing projects and networks, and was to help in the setting up of new projects. We agreed to set up a communications system incorporating a mailing list, a bulletin board system and a website, to run events and to work on producing a guide for publication.

Perusal of the notes taken at that meeting suggest that many of the ideas proposed then still hold good, and many of the proposals are being implemented through different routes and organizations: P4T fulfilled its role as catalyst; Communities Online became the focus for local networking; Richard Stubbs set up UK Citizens Online Democracy; David Wilcox is now running Partnerships Online and The Community Channel with emphasis on national networks (more on those later).

BT connections

In parallel with these nascent non-profit initiatives in 1995/96, Dave Greenop and colleagues in BT began serious research into the commercial potential for local community networking. This work at BT Labs was to be led by Colin Millar and Doug Williams, who became powerful allies in the years that followed and would later extend their work to Europe. In the long term, it may be that the most important influence on telecommunications development came through these early informal contacts with BT and later with GPT/Marconi.

After the October seminar - where we had gathered more support from practitioners - BT invited us to make a more substantial proposal to them. Mainly through the diligent business planning work of Richard Stubbs, we were able to make the case for £18,000 to develop the Community Regeneration Network. Again NCVO were able to help through a letter of endorsement, organized by Jonathon Brown in the rural team.

The Network was to be a bulletin-board system covering the development, management and funding of community-based projects for social, environmental and economic renewal.

We made great strides early in 1996 in using the FirstClass system to learn what would work and what wouldn't - but hit several snags. The main one was that we were ahead of the game: there weren't enough people involved in community-based regeneration online to achieve a critical mass of users. Planning Exchange already operated a similar system for local authorities, so we couldn't go for that more lucrative market, and we didn't have the resources to train new users. In addition, the World Wide Web was becoming the big attraction, and we did not have the funds to research and create a website as well as run a bulletin-board system, nor could we find anyone to provide us with low-cost facilities for e-mail lists.

Our technical needs were modest, and indeed must have seemed trivial to the people we were talking to in companies, universities and local authorities. Yet however much they sympathized, they could not offer us the facilities we needed while maintaining the essential security of their own systems. We were discovering that to innovate on the Net - even in modest ways - you need to control your own piece of cyberspace.

Further US connections

In Spring 1996 it was again the US connection which provided a way forward. David decided to take the plunge and finance a trip to the next community networking conference in the US. Doug Williams of BT Labs also made the trip. Steve Snow, director of Charlotte's Web, had floated the idea of an International Association for Community Networking (IACN) on the Communet mailing list, and a core group of us spent several months working the idea up online. David had to be there.

In the wonderful atmosphere of Taos, New Mexico, hosted this time by the local community network La Plaza, we hammered out plans for the association; David was coopted onto the working group – perhaps because an *international* association required a token non-American. He came back to the UK with the idea that we should set up the first national association for Community Networking, so steering Communities Online towards the promotion of local projects, rather than just leaving it as a national community of interest for regeneration practitioners.

Michael Mulquin and the steering group endorsed the idea, and Dave Miller at Sheffield University started the IACN mailing list, both as an aid to his pioneering academic research in the field, and as an essential communication tool for community networkers around the country.

(The International Association was never created. In practice we found that, despite the global reach of the Net, we needed to start within the country conventions of the 'real world'. The Americans later set up their own Association For Community Networking.)

Communities Online

Dave Miller also provided an opportunity to fly the flag for Communities Online at its June conference with an official announcement. We now had a real constituency of support. Shortly afterwards, a further meeting of the steering group endorsed the decision to set up a charitable company and create a shadow board chaired by Michael Mulquin. His employers, Aston Charities, agreed to hold the money until the company was formally set up - a vitally important function.

We agreed that a Communities Online Forum website should be set up, hosted initially on BT servers, and that a logo should be commissioned and a prospectus written as the first official publicity for the new organization. The funds for this were to come from BT Labs (thanks to Colin Miller and Doug Williams) and the Government's new IT for All initiative.

At this time we had three possible areas of activity. First was the development of special-interest networks - like the community regeneration initiative that we had started earlier. Secondly, there were local community networks, and thirdly, there was the networking of existing non-profit organizations whose members, it was felt, would play roles in both special-interest networks and local networks.

Later these different activities were to be promoted and supported through different organizations, with Communities Online focusing on local communities.

Before that happened, we were able to do some work with another of the key figures in the development of community networking: Kevin Harris of the Community Development Foundation. Kevin had researched and reported on the use of information and communication technologies in community and voluntary organizations for several years, and was able to secure funds from the Voluntary Services Unit at the Home Office for a 'Getting Connected' project. We ran demonstration days, a seminar, and created advisory material on the Web.

In addition, Kevin was secretary to the IBM-supported working party on social inclusion in the information society. The INSINC report,[1] published in June 1997, provided strong endorsement for community resource centres and networks, and became recognized as the key policy document in the field. Kevin was also later able to open the door for IBM support for Communities Online.

When New Labour became the Government on 1 May 1997, we were well prepared with new ideas, and found a receptive audience at the Department of Trade and Industry. We did not quite make it for 2 May, but we were through the door for a meeting on 8 May.

IT for all

On 9 May we made the following proposal:

Communities Online can help develop 'local IT for All' – a new dimension to the campaign will show the social and economic benefits of information and communication technologies in towns, cities and rural areas, and its relevance to people's day to day lives.

Communities Online will do this by developing a 'learning network' of the many innovative initiatives now under way – digital cities, virtual towns and community networks.[2]

In August the DTI were able to confirm that we had £87,000 to carry out our proposals – having made many helpful hints beforehand to keep our spirits up. By that time we had set new mailing lists with the help of David Fitzpatrick at Computer Access, built our website, contacted a wide range of local projects, and consolidated our national partnerships.

When IBM launched its report on Social Inclusion in the Information Society,[1] they invited us to join in the presentations and also to put forward funding proposals. As well as a cash and equipment, IBM seconded Samantha Hellawell, their Community Programmes Manager, for three days a week. Samantha began to make a contribution in Autumn 1997, and became a core member of the Communities Online team from January 1998.

The second Sheffield Conference for Community Information Networks in July 1997 provided the opportunity to launch Communities Online formally, and also brought another key contact: Nigel Worthington of the international communications company GPT (now Marconi) was researching community networks, and when some 40 conference participants decided they needed a venue for a further event, Nigel was able to offer the excellent facilities of a training centre in Dunchurch. He had asked rather tentatively whether 'community' networkers would take up such an offer from a commercial company, and had received strong reassurance that cross-partnerships were at the heart of our thinking.

Later on Nigel's boss, Paul Leidecker, was to become another strong supporter of Communities Online both morally and financially. It helped that he already knew the BT Labs team professionally. Corporate philanthropy was working in parallel with commercial research and development, with the prospect of genuine community and commercial benefit.

By autumn 1997, we felt we were on a roll, with a good team of part-time professionals and volunteer helpers drawn from Brighton, Newham and other projects. Peter Mason and Mark Walker from Sussex Community Internet Project were managing lists and upgrading the website. David Wilcox's wife Ann Holmes mapped out and managed a comprehensive programme of events, starting with a fringe meeting at the Labour Party conferences conveniently located just down the road on the Brighton seafront.

We were to find that the seminars on strategy and on specific topics were essential in building the network. It could not be done just online: face-to-face contact was essential to build relationships and spark new ideas. Fortunately this time the trips were only to York rather than to America.

To add an additional creative spark, David recruited longtime friend and colleague Drew Mackie to develop a community networking 'game' which would encourage groups to 'play' through the mix of technologies needed to support the social, economic and environmental development of a community.

Around the country, community networkers like Geoff Walker in Newcastle and Linda Doyle in Manchester lent their support and expertise through the many months when we wondered if we were on the right track. Geoff started on a map to chart the growth of networking projects throughout the country. We began to explore possible links with community radio and TV through Steve Buckley at the Community Media Association.

We were also drawing on the experience of Jane and Simon Berry, who had created the WREN telecottage near Coventry. Simon had been a key figure in the Telework, Telecottage and Telecentre Association, and was also director of the national Rural Enterprise Centre. He was eager to network rural communities and organizations - a dream realized when part of the IBM equipment donation provided a server for Ruralnet.

As Communities Online developed our excitement at the new possibilities was only slightly tempered by the realization that others had been there before us. Horace Mitchell, who later became chair of Communities Online, was programme director of European Telework Development, with unparalleled knowledge of European funding programmes and a rare genius for combining wit and wisdom in contributions to mailing lists.

Adrian Norman had worked in the Cabinet Office in the early 1980s during the first round of enthusiasm for community and educational computing. In the late 1990s he was developing a model for Internet gateway sites and databases that could carry both community information and the commercial content needed for sustainability. He even knew - and could explain - how e-commerce would work.

By the end of 1997 we had re-presented Communities Online as a campaign for community networking with three elements: advocacy, networking practitioners, and the development of innovative partnerships and projects.

Michael's greatest interest was in advocacy and networking practitioners, while David wanted to concentrate on new developments. It was time for reassessment of roles, and for David to recognize that he had more enthusiasm for starting initiatives than running organizations. So Michael became full-time Executive Director from January 1998, and David was to work for a few months on a consultancy basis while setting up Partnerships Online. This would provide some of the detailed 'how to' knowledge and tools for community networking, and would also develop other initiatives outside the remit of Communities Online.

Communities Online would continue to develop as a learning network of practitioners, and would also concentrate on awareness raising among decision makers of the importance of a locally based, socially inclusive information society. It would operate as a company.

During 1998 Partnerships Online developed as a loose network of individuals and organizations who wanted to 'mix and match' work on a number of projects. These included:

- developing guidance material on community resources centres with Jane Berry, and running a seminar on this with Unipart, where a team of graduate trainers had worked with the community to create a centre on a nearby estate, the Barton Hub
- organizing a UK tour for US community networker Terry Grunwald, with events in Sussex, London and Scotland.
- setting up Sussex Online to promote community networking on the south coast

- creating websites for a number of non-profit organizations, including the Development Trusts Association and Town and Country Planning Association
- developing, with Simon Berry and Peter Mason, a comprehensive communications system for the Community Action Network (CAN), led by Adele Blakebrough, which aims to connect 2000 social entrepreneurs by the end of the year 2000.

The most significant strategic work started in June 1998, when work started with CAN and CDF to gain the support of two government departments – the Home Office and the Department of Trade and Industry – and of about ten organizations, to a programme of activities called 'Making the Net Work' (in honour of Terry Grunwald's book of the same name[3]).

The main initiative to develop from this was The Community Channel, which received DTI and Home Office funding to create connections between practitioners and policy makers through events, e-mail and the Web around topics of social exclusion and regeneration.

During 1999 The Channel will be focusing on the role that information and communication technologies have in these fields. We hope this will yield policy insights and practical lessons, and also help create more links between the various national initiatives in the field.

This history shows how many people have been involved in developing community networking in the UK, how messy it has been, how dependent on chance connection, and how difficult to organize – just like the Internet.

Communities Online continues

Communities Online started off 1998 with a bang, running two 24-hour seminars in Harrogate, one on digital villages and the other on community resource centres. A number of other events took place:

- a one-day seminar looking at various software packages that would be useful for community networks, and also looking at the human skills needed to make them work effectively
- an awareness-raising event for business, which raised a lot of inter-

est a series of small focused presentations to key companies
- a one-day seminar looking at how local community-based ICT initiatives could contribute to local economic development.

The latter was the public launch of a process managed by Claire
Shearman to look into ICTs and economic regeneration in more detail,
which had been greatly helped by the secondment of Helen Ghosh,
Director of Regeneration for London East at the Government Office
for London. She spent three weeks full-time with Claire in September
1998, and as a result of their work Communities Online ran a one-day
seminar on regeneration funding and locally based ICT initiatives in
January 1999. We also commissioned Claire to build on the work she
had already done to develop a response to the report published by the
Government's Social Exclusion Unit on tackling the problems of
deprived neighbourhoods.[4]

Communities Online, which was set up as a not-for-profit company
limited by guarantee, held the 1998 Annual Conference in York, where
70 practitioners came together for two days to learn from and be
inspired by each other. The company's e-mail discussion list now has
over 170 participants representing over 80 different projects, and the list
is growing all the time. Because these are all local projects, there is a
great need for them to find ways to share their experiences and collab-
orate on common issues. We see this as being one of the central reasons
for Communities Online's existence.

The European Association for Community Networking

The seeds for this idea came from two initiatives that happened in 1997.
BCNet from Spain and Rete Civica Net from Italy cooperated to
organize the first European Conference for Community Networks in
Milan in July. Vecam in France organized an event in September
focused on Parthenay, a town that had set itself the goal of utilising the
new technologies to the full. As the preparations for these two events
went ahead, it became obvious that it would make sense to ensure
proper coordination between them. Because of this, 12 people involved
in community networking initiatives in seven different countries met

in Brussels in June for a day to start the discussions for a Europe-wide initiative. As a result of this meeting, proposals to set up a European Association for Community Networks were drawn up. These were put to those attending the Milan conference, who enthusiastically endorsed them. Unfortunately, everyeone was too busy subsequently to take the idea forward any further, although a presentation was made to the conference in Parthenay.

In July 1998 the second European Community Networks conference was held in Barcelona, and once again the idea of setting up a European Association received a very positive response. This time six of us put ourselves forward, and made ourselves accountable to the delegates for putting together a draft constitution for wide circulation and raising funds to set the organization up. We have put together a simple draft constitution, and will be setting up as an international association registered in Belgium. We have obtained initial funding which will enable us formally to register the organization, to pay for the design of a logo and the printing of a leaflet in several European languages, and to have our first small conference of about 30 participants to develop a clear structure and work programme. So the future looks really bright.

References

1   The net result: social inclusion in the information society: report of the National Working Party on Social Inclusion (INSINC), IBM UK and CDF, 1997. Available at
     <http://www.uk.ibm.com/comm/community/uk117.html>

2   <http://www.communities.org.uk>
     This site has many connecting links and information resources.

3   Grunwald, T., Making the Net work: online strategies for community-based organisations, North Carolina, NCexChange, 1997. Available from NCexChange, PO Box 28068, Raleigh, NC 27611-8068, USA. Published and available also in the UK by Partnerships Online, 13 Pelham Square, Brighton BN1 4ET, UK. Tel/Fax: +44 (0)1273 677377; e-mail: david@communities.org.uk.
     <http://www.partnerships.org.uk>

4   Social Exclusion Unit, Bringing Britain together, 1998.

Appendix 1: Bibliography

Further reading and researching

As this is a constantly changing scene, the following are listed to enable the reader to obtain an overview of worldwide developments. The websites listed demonstrate a wide variety in the aims and objectives, and using some of the websites listed below, many more sources are available.

Bajaly, Stephen, *The community networking handbook*, American Library Association, ALA Editions, 1999, ISBN 0 8389 745 8.

Information Society Forum, *Networks for people and their communities: making most of the information society in the European Union*. First annual report to the European Commission, June 1996. Cordis Focus, 15 September 1996, Supplement Number 10. Office for Official Publications of the European Communities, L-2985 Luxembourg.

Ormes, Sarah, and Dempsey, Lorcan (eds), *The Internet, networking and the public library*, Library Association Publishing in association with the UK Office for Library and Information Networking, University of Bath, 1997. ISBN 1 85604 202 2.

Partnerships Online lists the following publications:
Guide to effective participation;
Guide to development trusts and partnerships;
Inventing the future; and
How to use IT in the community.
All the above publications available on the website
<http://www.partnerships.org.uk/pubs/index.htm>

World Wide Web sources

<http://www.lights.com/freenet/>
Go to this website for a listing of Free-Nets/Community information networks around the world, covering the following countries: Australia, Austria, Canada, Finland, Germany, Hungary, Israel, Italy, Netherlands, Russia, Spain, Ukraine, United Kingdom and the Unites States.

The following are also of interest: all have their own aims and objectives and serve as models for anyone starting their own community information network in the many areas they cover. There are many more community information networks which can be found by linking into these sites.

CANADA

<http://www.oise.on.ca/~skarsten/community.html>
Communities and the Internet list a number of sites, which demonstrate the variety of 'communities' now active on the Internet.

UK

<amazon.co.uk>
Amazon Books UK is a constantly updated online source of titles from worldwide publishers; it gives a short list of available titles on community networks.

<http://panizzi.shef/ac.uk/colweb>
Barnsley College of the Web aims to increase skills and experience in IT and Internet usage in the Barnsley area, aimed particularly, amongst others, at community organizations in the area.

<http://www.blink.org.uk>
Black Information Link, London acts as a forum and provides information to bring about improvements in race relations.

<http://www.brixton.co.uk>
Brixton On-Line offers opportunities for organizations in the area.

<http://www.buchanweb.demon.co.uk>
Buchan Community Web serves the people of Central Buchan in the North East of Scotland.

<http://www.worldserver.pipex.com/cambndge/>
Cambridge City site serves people in a wide area, listing events, facilities and services.

<http://www.cardiff.ac.uk/ccin/homepage.html>
Capital Cardiff Netlists: what's on, news, information about Cardiff, business and other services.

<http://www.charitynet.org/index.html>
Charities Aid Foundation web services: CharityNet has a search engine listing over 70,000 community groups, links to Corporate Community Involvement Pages on company websites and the CharityCard Directory.

<http:/www.charity-commission.gov.uk>
Charity Commission website.

<http://www.cdf.org.uk>
Communities Development Foundation focuses on social inclusion, regeneration and other topics for the community sector. An extensive list of books is offered, some free of charge from CDF: see http://www.cdf.org.uk/Publications_list htm.
Current literature and photocopies are available for a small fee.
<http://www.cdf.org uk/currlit.htm>

<http://www.communities.org.uk>
Communities Online for those seeking to use technologies to benefit their communities.

<http://www/cwn.orgluk/index.html
Coventry and Warwickshire website, set up and run by Chris Studman, is a very successful community information network, offering a very wide range of services.

<http://www.ccis.org.uk/dataldata.html>
Craigmillar in Scotland services a deprived area of Edinburgh and lists other initiatives in the area.

<http://www.dearnevalley.org.uk/>
Dearne Valley Online established a partnership with schools, libraries and other agencies in the Dearne Valley in Yorkshire to pilot the use of Internet links in the community on a trial basis for the evaluation of practical issues about linking distributed communities to online information and learning facilities.

<http://www.derwentside.org.uk/>
The Derwentside Infonet Community site aims to provide better access to information, improve communications between organizations and raise awareness of IT within the area.

<http://www.zynet.co.uk/base/deldaf/>
Devon Local Development Agencies Forum (Deldaf) offers a range of information, local news, training, jobs, and funding sources.

<http://www.disabilitynet.co.uk>
DisabilityNet is an information, discussion and news service for disabled people and those with an interest in disability issues.

<http://www.barnsley.org.uk/>
Grimethorpe Electronic Village Hall Ltd (GEVH) started life with no resources but plenty of enthusiasm from its workers. It is now regarded as an excellent example of what can be achieved in a deprived community.

<http://www.handsworth.org.uk>
Handsworth Electronic Community Network (HECNET) services the community of Handsworth in Sheffield, Yorkshire. It has a range of services on offer, and is supported by the European Social Fund.

<http://www.nrec.org.ik/inforurale>
InfoRurale Information gateway for rural development, is part of the National Rural Enterprise Council.

<http://www.madeley.org.uk/index.htm>
Madeley, South Telford offers a range of services from Citizens Advice
Bureaux. It has a library, voluntary services and much more.

<http://www.mailbase.org.uk>
Mailbase is an electronic discussion list for the UK higher education
community, but is open to others.

<http://www.manor-castle.org.uk/>
Manor and Castle area of Sheffield website is the result of a partnership
of local organizations to provide people in the area with access to
information and resources about the locality.

<http://users.powernet.co.uk/mkcw>
Milton Keynes Community Web is a small voluntary organization set
up to help voluntary organizations in the area make effective use of the
World Wide Web and the Internet.

<http://www.newtel.org.uk/>
Newham Borough, in the East End of London promotes the use of the
Internet among voluntary and community organizations. It is part of
the Community Involvement Unit of Aston Charities Trust.

<http://www.nacn.org/>

<http://www.nics.gov.uk/cinnilindex.htm>

<http://www.oneworld.org/community.web/index1.html>
One World, run in partnership with British Telecommunications Ltd,
provides free web services for the UK public and for organizations from
the community and voluntary sectors.

<http://www.partnerships.org.uk>
Partnerships Online lists a wealth of information, including partnerships, projects, publications, organizations, frequently asked questions,
glossary, events, links to UK and international organizations, who's
who and much more.

<http://www.poptel.netsales/>
Poptel is a co-op set up to provide Internet access and publishing services for non-profit organizations including major trades unions, the UK Labour Party and voluntary sector organizations.

<http://dspace.dial.pipe.com/town/square/ac940/weblibs.html>
A list of public libraries and other resources, compiled by Sheila and Robert Harden.

<http://www.webserve.co.uk/clients/saffire/>
Saffron Walden, Thaxted, Great Dunmow in the district of Uttlesford provides a wealth of information from community services to history, customs and legends.

<http://www.school-net.org.uk/intro.html>
School-Net from the City School, Sheffield is another example of what a community website can offer. The objective was to set up a charitable company to sell Internet accounts which would provide schools and their communities with the revenue to make quality access to information and communications technology (ICT) available to all.

<http://www.e-base.org.uk/>
Tower Hamlets Community in London is constructed by volunteers to enable community-based computer networks be achieved.

<http://www.spin.org.uk>
The Society of Public Information Networks (SPIN) is now long established and provides information about local authorities offering information electronically. There is a list of member organizations.

<http://panizzi.shef.ac.uk/community>
The University of Sheffield, Department of Information Studies extensive site is run by David Miller, the Department's Computer Manager, who has encouraged many organizations to start their own community information network. It has links also to other sites, national and international, coordinating bodies, further readings, mailing lists and newsletters, and research projects.

<http://www.vois.org..uk>
Voluntary Organizations Internet Server (VOIS) offers a resource centre, a volunteers' noticeboard and a searchable database community.

<http://www.community-work-training.org.uk>
West Yorkshire Community Training Group site, includes training materials, articles and links.

USA

<amazon.com>
Amazon Books USA is a constantly updated source of books from worldwide publishers; it gives a short list of available titles on community networks.

<http://bcn.boulder.co.us/afcn/>
The Association for Community Networking provides details of the association, benefits and primary participants

<http://www.benton.org/Cyber/>
The Benton Foundation, Washington DC lists a selection of resources on the Internet. It also has 'Benton Best Practices Toolkit' of resources aimed at helping non-profitmaking organizations use communications technology.

<http://macsky.bigsky.dillon.mt.us/community.html>
Big Sky Telegraph's website, connecting rural Montana, USA to the world, has extensive links to national and international directories, resources, guidelines, best community network models and much more.

<http://morino.org/>
The Morino Institute in the United States aims to help people to improve their lives and communities.

<http://www.nptn.org/>
The National Public Telecomputing Network in the United States is

the parent body for Free-Net systems worldwide.

<http://www.si.umich.edu/Community/about.html>

The University of Michigan, *Community Connector website* lists the mission, goals, and objectives. It includes an extensive list of online papers relating to community information systems which can be obtained by author or date. <http://archimedes.si.umich.edu/cfdocs/community/RRbyYear.cfm>

Appendix 2: Glossary

Acronyms, initials and other words are constantly being invented in the Internet/ Community information network world. See also the various websites and other references in the reading lists at the end of the chapters and in Appendix 1 Further reading and researching.

ACN	Association for Community Networking
ADN	advanced digital network
ASCII	American standard code for information interchange
BBS	bulletin board system
BCNet	Barcelona Community Network
bookmark	allows the user to bookmark a web site for future reference
BRI	basic rate interface
BT	British Telecom
CAB	Citizens Advice Bureaux
CANet	Centre for Internet Applications, Barcelona
CDF	Community Development Foundation
CD-ROM	compact disc read only memory
CIN	community information network
CGI	common gateway interface
CRC	community resource centre
CSCL	computer supported collaborative learning
cyberspace	word used to describe information resources available via computer networks
domain name	unique name indicating the Internet site of an organization
EARL	Electronic Access to Resources in and through Libraries
e-mail	electronic mail which can be sent worldwide

	between people and organizations. Perhaps the most used part of the Internet
ESF	European Social Fund
EU	European Union
FAQs	frequently asked questions which are asked on a particular subject
FE	further education
ftp	file transfer protocol
GEVH	Grimethorpe Electronic Village Hall Ltd
gif	graphical interface format, used for picture transfer
GILS	Government Information Locator Service
HCF	Handsworth Community Forum
HE	higher education
HECNET	Handsworth Electronic Community Network
home page	the first page seen when a web site is entered
HTML	hypertext markup language
HTTP	hypertext transport protocol
IACN	International Association for Community Networking
ICAS	Internet civic address service
ICT	information communication technologies
IP	Internet protocol
IPA	Internet professional address
IRC	Internet relay chat
ISDN	integrated services digital networks
ISP	Internet service provider
IT	information technology
JPEG	Joint Photographic Expert Group
LAN	local area network
LISTSERV	mailing list management system
MIME	MultiPurpose Internet Mail Extensions which allows files to be attached to emails so that the files can be transferred between computers
MODEM	MODulator/DEModulator, a device to connect computer to a telephone to allow communication with other computers

NCVO	National Council for Voluntary Organizations
NGI	next generation Internet
NGO	Non-Governmental Organization
NPO	Non-Profit Organization
OPAC	online public access catalogue
P4T	Partnerships for Tomorrow
PAT	policy action team
POP	point of presence service which allows a connection to the Internet. Also known as Post Office Protocol.
PPP	point to point protocol
RAIN	Rotherham Advice and Information Network
RMBC	Rotherham Metropolitan Borough Council
RNIB	Royal National Institute for the Blind
Service Provider	organizations providing access to the Internet and the associated services
SEU	Social Exclusion Unit
SGML	standardized markup language
TCP/IP	transmission control protocol/Internet protocol
TEC	Training and Enterprise Council
UKOLN	United Kingdom Office for Library and Information Networking
UPC	Universitat Politechnica de Catalunya
URL	uniform resource locator – address for a website
VIP	village information point
WAN	wide area network which covers a large area, e.g. a university campus
WWW	World Wide Web
WYSIWIG	what you see is what you get

Index